WATCHMEN

ALAN MOORE
writer

DAVE GIBBONS
illustrator / letterer

JOHN HIGGINS
colorist

Published by DC Comics.
1700 Broadway, New York, NY 10019.
Cover and hardcover compilation
Copyright © 2008 DC Comics.
All rights reserved. Originally published in single
magazine form as WATCHMEN 1-12 © 1986, 1987
DC Comics. All rights reserved. All characters, their
distinctive likenesses and related elements featured
in this publication are trademarks of DC Comics.
The stories, characters, and incidents mentioned in
this publication are entirely fictional. Printed on
recyclable paper. DC Comics does not read or accept
unsolicited submissions of ideas, stories or artwork.
Printed in USA. First Printing.
ISBN: 978-1-4012-1926-0

DC Comics, a Warner Bros. Entertainment Company.

Original Publication, Conceptual Art and Design
by Dave Gibbons

Original Publication Design by Julia Sabbagh

Original Graphitti Edition Design
by Bob Chapman and Jessie Horsting

DC COMICS

DAN DIDIO
Senior VP-Executive Editor
LEN WEIN & BARBARA RANDALL
Editors-Original Series
BOB HARRAS
Editor-Collected Edition
ROBBIN BROSTERMAN
Senior Art Director
PAUL LEVITZ
President & Publisher
GEORG BREWER
VP-Design & DC Direct Creative
RICHARD BRUNING
Senior VP-Creative Director
PATRICK CALDON
Executive VP-Finance & Operations
CHRIS CARAMALIS
VP-Finance
JOHN CUNNINGHAM
VP-Marketing
TERRI CUNNINGHAM
VP-Managing Editor
AMY GENKINS
Senior VP-Business & Legal Affairs
ALISON GILL
VP-Manufacturing
DAVID HYDE
VP-Publicity
HANK KANALZ
VP-General Manager, WildStorm
JIM LEE
Editorial Director-WildStorm
GREGORY NOVECK
Senior VP-Creative Affairs
SUE POHJA
VP-Book Trade Sales
STEVE ROTTERDAM
Senior VP-Sales & Marketing
CHERYL RUBIN
Senior VP-Brand Management
ALYSSE SOLL
VP-Advertising & Custom Publishing
JEFF TROJAN
VP-Business Development, DC Direct
BOB WAYNE
VP-Sales

Original Color 1986; additional Coloring
& Digital Finishing 2005 by John Higgins

Art Reconstruction by:
Hank Manfra
Aaron Tappen
Emily Ryan Lerner
Corey Breen

Color Reconstruction
by WildStorm FX:
Carrie Strachan
Randy Mayor
Darlene Royer
David Rodriguez

With special thanks to
Neil Gaiman, Mike Lake,
Pat Mills, and Joe Orlando.

CHAPTER I

SO LOOK, YOU HAVEN'T ANSWERED MY **QUESTION**... IS THIS A **BURGLARY**, OR DO WE LOOK FOR SOME **OTHER** MOTIVE?

LISTEN, IT **COULD** JUST HAVE BEEN A BURGLARY... MAYBE A BUNCH 'A **KNOT-TOPS** ON **KT-28**s OR **'LUUDES**...

"YOU KNOW HOW IT IS... A LOT OF CRAZY THINGS HAPPEN IN A CITY THIS SIZE.

"THEY DON'T **ALL** NEED MOTIVES."

SO, WHAT YOU'RE **SAYING** IS...

I'M **SAYING** LET'S NOT RAISE TOO MUCH **DUST** OVER THIS ONE. WE DON'T NEED ANY **MASKED AVENGERS** GETTING INTERESTED AND **CUTTING IN**.

FOLLOW IT UP **DISCREETLY**, SURE. BUT IN **PUBLIC**...

"...WELL, WHAT SAY WE LET THIS ONE DROP OUT OF **SIGHT**?"

I DUNNO. I THINK YOU TAKE THIS **VIGILANTE** STUFF TOO **SERIOUSLY**. SINCE THE **KEENE ACT** WAS PASSED IN '77, ONLY THE **GOVERNMENT-SPONSORED WEIRDOS** ARE ACTIVE.

THEY DON'T INTERFERE.

SCREW THEM. WHAT ABOUT **RORSCHACH**?

"**RORSCHACH** NEVER RETIRED, EVEN AFTER HIM AND HIS BUDDIES FELL OUTTA GRACE.

"RORSCHACH'S STILL **OUT** THERE SOMEWHERE."

HE'S CRAZIER THAN A SNAKE'S ARMPIT AND WANTED ON TWO COUNTS **MURDER ONE**.

WE GOT A COZY LITTLE **HOMICIDE** HERE. IF **HE** GETS INVOLVED, WE'LL BE UP TO OUR **BUTTS** IN **CORPSES**...

WHAT'S THE **MATTER**?

UH, NOTHING ...JUST A **SHIVER**.

MUST BE GETTIN' A **COLD**.

4

AT MIDNIGHT, ALL THE AGENTS...

HURM.

8

SO, THERE I WAS IN THE SUPERMARKET BUYIN' *DOGFOOD* FOR OL' *PHANTOM* HERE, I TURN THE CORNER OF THE AISLE AND *WHAM!* I BUMP INTO THE *SCREAMING SKULL!*

YOU *REMEMBER* HIM?

I THINK I HEARD YOU *MENTION* HIM...

OH, I PUT HIM AWAY A DOZEN TIMES IN THE *FORTIES*, BUT HE *REFORMED* AN' TURNED TO *JESUS* SINCE THEN. MARRIED, GOT TWO KIDS...

WE TRADED ADDRESSES. NICE GUY.

UH, HOLLIS, LISTEN... IT'S ALMOST MIDNIGHT. I OUGHTTA *GO*.

OH, SURE. LOST TRACK O' THE TIME THERE, TALKIN' 'BOUT ALL THAT OLD STUFF.

YOU MUSTA BEEN BORED AS HELL.

YOU KNOW BETTER THAN *THAT*. THESE SATURDAY NIGHT *BEER SESSIONS* ARE WHAT KEEPS ME *GOING*.

YEAH, WELL, US OLD RETIRED GUYS GOTTA STICK TOGETHER.

LEMME PUT THIS OUT AND I'LL BE RIGHT WITH YA.

Y'KNOW, IT WAS A CRYIN' SHAME THEY PUT YOU YOUNGSTERS OUT TO GRASS IN '77. YOU WERE A BETTER *NITE OWL* THAN I *EVER* WAS.

HOLLIS, WE *BOTH* KNOW THAT'S BULLSHIT, BUT THANKS *ANYWAY*.

HEY, WATCH WITH THE *LANGUAGE!* THIS IS THE LEFT HOOK THAT FLOORED *CAPTAIN AXIS*, REMEMBER?

HOW COULD I *FORGET*. THANKS FOR ANOTHER GREAT NIGHT, HOLLIS. TAKE *CARE* OF YOURSELF.

YOU *TOO*, DANNY.

GOD BLESS.

9

...LOOK DOWN YOUR BACK STAIRS, BUDDY, SOMEBODY'S LIVING THERE AN' THEY DON'T REALLY FEEL THE WEATHER...

SHORP.

LEP.

HELLO, DANIEL.

CHLOP.

THLUP.

GOT HUNGRY WAITING. HELPED MYSELF TO SOME BEANS.

HOPE YOU DON'T MIND.

RORSCHACH..?

10

H-HEY! HEY, I DIDN'T **MEAN** ANYTHING...

I, UH, I HAVEN'T **BEEN** IN THE APPLE TOO LONG, AND I...

...I, UH...

HEY, WHAT...?

AAAAA

I'VE JUST BROKEN THIS GENTLEMAN'S LITTLE FINGER.

WHO KILLED EDWARD BLAKE?

OH. OUHH...

EEYIIAAA

...AND HIS INDEX FINGER.

WHO KILLED EDWARD BLAKE?

PLEASE...

PLEASE, WE DON'T **KNOW**...

AW, **GOD**, MAN, LEAVE HIM **ALONE**...

FIRST VISIT OF EVENING FRUITLESS. NOBODY KNEW ANYTHING. FEEL SLIGHTLY DEPRESSED.

THIS CITY IS DYING OF RABIES. IS THE BEST I CAN DO TO WIPE RANDOM FLECKS OF FOAM FROM ITS LIPS?

HURM.

never despair. never surrender.

I LEAVE THE HUMAN COCKROACHES TO DISCUSS THEIR HEROIN AND CHILD PORNOGRAPHY. I HAVE BUSINESS ELSEWHERE, WITH A BETTER CLASS OF PERSON.

16

YOU SEEM TO BE UPSETTING *LAURIE.*

I THINK YOU OUGHT TO GO.

WITH RESPECT, DR. MANHATTAN, I WARNED VEIDT AND DREIBERG AND I INTEND TO WARN YOU AND YOUR LADY FRIEND.

I BELIEVE SOMEONE IS ELIMINATING MASKED ADVENTURERS, POSSIBLY SOME OLD FOE WITH A GRUDGE. I BELIEVE...

I SAID I THINK YOU OUGHT TO GO.

SPENT A LOT OF TIME GETTING IN TO SEE YOU.

NOT LEAVING BEFORE I'VE...

...HAD MY SAY.

HURM.

22

WELL, I GUESS IT'S GETTING PRETTY LATE.

IT'S BEEN A GREAT EVENING, LAURIE. YOU'RE SURE YOU WON'T LET ME PICK UP THE TAB?

NAH. IF I'M GONNA BE A KEPT WOMAN FOR THE MILITARY'S SECRET WEAPON, THEN THE MILITARY CAN STAND ME A BOWL OF SPAGHETTI AFRICAINE EVERY ONCE IN A WHILE.

HEY, YOU SOUND BITTER.

NO. NOT REALLY. IT'S JUST THAT THE ONLY REASON I'M KEPT AROUND IS TO KEEP JON RELAXED AND HAPPY.

UH... IS EVERYTHING OKAY WITH YOU AND JON?

Rafael's

ME AND JON?

OH, YEAH. YEAH, EVERYTHING'S FINE.

COULDN'T BE BETTER.

IT'S JUST I KEEP THINKING "I'M THIRTY-FIVE. WHAT HAVE I DONE?"

I'VE SPENT EIGHT YEARS IN SEMI-RETIREMENT, PRECEDED BY TEN YEARS RUNNING ROUND IN A STUPID COSTUME BECAUSE MY STUPID MOTHER WANTED ME TO!

YOU REMEMBER THAT COSTUME?

WITH THAT STUPID LITTLE SHORT SKIRT AND THE NECKLINE GOING DOWN TO MY NAVEL? GOD, THAT WAS SO DREADFUL.

GOD, YES. DREADFUL.

Y'KNOW, WHEN I THINK BACK... WHY DID WE DO IT? WHY DID WE DRESS UP LIKE THAT?

THE KEENE ACT WAS THE BEST THING THAT EVER HAPPENED TO US.

YEAH. YOU'RE PROBABLY RIGHT.

25

UNDER THE HOOD

We present here excerpts from Hollis Mason's autobiography, UNDER THE HOOD, leading up to the time when he became the masked adventurer, Nite Owl. Reprinted with permission of the author.

I.

The lady who works in the grocery store at the corner of my block is called Denise, and she's one of America's great unpublished novelists. Over the years she's written *forty-two* romantic novels, none of which have ever reached the bookstores. I, however, have been fortunate enough to hear the plots of the last twenty-seven of these recounted in installments by the authoress herself every time I drop by the store for a jar of coffee or can of beans, and my respect for Denise's literary prowess knows no bounds. So, naturally enough, when I found myself faced with the daunting task of actually starting the book you now hold in your hands, it was Denise I turned to for advice.

"Listen," I said. "I don't know from writing a book. I have all this stuff in my head that I want to get down, but what do I write about first? Where do I begin?"

Without looking up from the boxes of detergent to which she was fixing price tags, Denise graciously delivered up a pearl of her accumulated wisdom in a voice of bored but benign condescension.

"Start off with the saddest thing you can think of and get the audience's sympathies on your side. After that, believe me, it's a walk."

Thank you, Denise. This book is dedicated to you, because I don't know how to choose between all the other people I should be dedicating it to.

The saddest thing I can think of is "The Ride of the Valkyries." Every time I hear it I get depressed and start wondering about the lot of humanity and the unfairness of life and all those other things that you think about at three in the morning when your digestion won't let you sleep. Now, I realize that nobody else on the planet has to brush away a tear when they hear that particular stirring refrain, but that's because they don't know about Moe Vernon.

When my father upped and left my Granddad's farm in Montana to bring his family to New York, Moe Vernon was the man he worked for. Vernon's Auto Repairs was just off Seventh Avenue, and although it was only 1928 when Dad started working there, there was just about enough trade for his wages to keep me and Mom and my sister Liantha in food and clothing. Dad was always really keen and enthusiastic about his work, and I used to think it was just because he had a thing about cars. Looking back, I can see it was more than that. It must have meant so much to him, just to have a job and be able to support his family. He'd had a lot of arguments with his father about coming east rather than taking over the farm, like the old man had planned for him, and most of the rows had ended with my grandfather predicting poverty and moral ruination for my dad and mom if they so much as set foot in New York. To be living the life that he himself had chosen and keeping his family above the poverty line in spite of his father's warnings must have meant more to my dad than anything in the world, but that's something I only understand now, with hindsight. Back then, I just thought he was crazy for crankshafts.

Anyway, I was twelve years old when we left Montana, so during those next few years in the big city I was just the age to appreciate the occasional trips to the auto shop with my dad, which is where I first set eyes on Moe Vernon, his employer.

Moe Vernon was a man around fifty-five or so, and he had one of those old New York faces that you don't see anymore. It's funny, but certain faces seem to go in and out of style. You look at old photographs and everybody has a certain look to them, almost as if they're related. Look at pictures from ten years later and you can see that there's a new kind of face starting to predominate, and that the old faces are fading away and vanishing, never to be seen again. Moe Vernon's face was like that: three chins, a wiseacre cynical curl to his lower lip, a certain hollowness around the eyes, hair retreating back across his head, attempting a rendezvous with the label on his shirt collar.

Vernon's Auto Repair c. 1928. (left to right) My father; myself, age 12; Moe Vernon; Fred Motz.

I'd go into the shop with my dad and Moe would be sitting there in his office, which had glass sides so he could watch the men working. Sometimes, if my father wanted to check something out with Moe before going ahead with his work, he'd send me over to the office to do it for him, which meant that I got to see the insides of Moe's inner sanctum. Or rather, I got to hear them.

You see, Moe was an opera buff. He had one of the new gramophones over in the corner of his office and all day he used to play scratchy old seventy-eight recordings of his favorites just as loud as he could manage. By today's standard, "as loud as he could manage" didn't amount to a whole lot of noise, but it sounded pretty cacophonous back in 1930, when things were generally quieter.

The other thing that was peculiar about Moe was his sense of humor, as represented by all the stuff he used to keep in the top right side drawer of his desk.

In that drawer, amongst a mess of rubber bands and paper clips and receipts and stuff, Moe had one of the largest collections of tasteless novelty items that I had seen up until that point or have seen at any time since. They were all risqué little toys and gadgets that Moe had picked up from gag shops or on visits to Coney Island, but it was the sheer range of them that was overwhelming: every cheap blue gimmick that you can remember your dad bringing home when he'd been out drinking with the boys and embarrassing your mom with; every ballpoint pen with a girl on the side whose swimsuit vanished when you turned it upside down; every salt and pepper crewet set shaped like a woman's breasts; every plastic dog mess. Moe had the works. Every time anybody went into his office he'd try to startle them by displaying his latest plaything. Actually, it used to shock my dad more than it did me. I don't think he liked the idea of his son being exposed to that kind of stuff, probably because of all the moral warnings my grandfather had impressed upon him. For my part, I wasn't offended and I even found it kind of funny. Not the things themselves . . . even by then I was too old to get much amusement out of stuff like that. What I found funny was that for no apparent reason, a grown man should have a desk drawer full of such ludicrous devices.

Anyway, one day in 1933, a little after my seventeenth birthday, I was over at Vernon's Auto Repairs with Dad, helping him poke around in the oily innards of a busted-up Ford. Moe was in his office, and although we didn't find out till later, he was sitting wearing an artificial foam rubber set of realistically painted lady's bosoms, with which he hoped to get a few laughs from the guy who brought him the morning mail through from the front office when it arrived. While he waited, he was listening to Wagner.

The mail arrived in due course, and the guy handing it over managed to raise a dutiful chuckle at Moe's generous cleavage before leaving him to open and peruse the morning's missives. Amongst these (again, as we found out later) there was a letter from Moe's wife Beatrice, informing him that for the past two years she'd been sleeping with Fred Motz, the senior and most trusted mechanic employed at Vernon's Auto Repairs, who, unusually, hadn't shown up for work on that particular morning. This, according to the concluding paragraphs of the letter, was because Beatrice had taken all the money out of the joint account she shared with her husband and had departed with Fred for Tijuana.

The first anyone in the workshop knew about this was when the door of Moe's office slammed open and the startlingly loud and crackling rendition of "Ride of the Valkyries" blasted out from within. Framed in the doorway with tears in his eyes and the crumpled letter in his hand, Moe stood dramatically with all eyes turned towards him. He was still wearing the set of artificial breasts. Almost inaudible above the rising strains of Wagner swelling behind him, he spoke, with so much hurt and outrage and offended dignity fighting for possession of his voice that the end result was almost toneless.

"Fred Motz has had carnal knowledge of my wife Beatrice for the past two years."

He stood there in the wake of his announcement, the tears rolling down over his multiple chins to soak into the pink foam rubber of his bosom, making tiny sounds in his chest and throat that were trampled under the hooves of the Valkyries and lost forever.

And everybody started laughing.

I don't know what it was. We could see he was crying, but it was just something in the toneless way he'd said it, standing there wearing a pair of false breasts with all that crashing, triumphant music soaring all around him. None of us could help it, laughing at him like that. My dad and I were both doubled up and the other guys slaving over the nearby cars were wiping tears from their eyes and smearing their faces with oil in the process. Moe just looked at us all for a minute and then went back into his office and closed the door. A moment or two later the Wagner stopped with an ugly scraping noise as Moe snatched the needle from the groove of the gramophone record, and after that there was silence.

About half an hour passed before someone went in to apologize on behalf of everybody and to see if Moe was all right. Moe accepted the apology and said that he was fine. Apparently he was sitting there at his desk, breasts now discarded, getting on with normal routine paperwork as if nothing had happened.

I graduate from Police Academy (1938)

That night, he sent everybody home early. Then, running a tube from the exhaust of one of the shop's more operational vehicles in through the car's window, he started up the engine and drifted off into a final, bitter sleep amongst the carbon monoxide fumes. His brother took over the business and even eventually reemployed Fred Motz as chief mechanic.

And that's why "The Ride of the Valkyries" is the saddest thing I can think of, even though it's somebody else's tragedy rather than my own. I was there and I laughed along with all the rest and I guess that makes it part of my story too.

Now, if Denise's theory is correct, I should have your full sympathy and the rest will be a walk. So maybe it's safe to tell you about all the stuff you probably bought this book to read about. Maybe it's safe to tell you why I'm crazier than Moe Vernon ever was. I didn't have a drawer full of erotic novelties, but I guess I had my own individual quirks. And although I've never worn a set of false bosoms in my life, I've stood there dressed in something just as strange, with tears in my eyes while people died laughing.

II.

By 1939 I was twenty-three years old and had taken a job on the New York City police force. I've never really examined until now just why I should have chosen that particular career, but I guess it came as a result of a number of things. Foremost amongst these was probably my grandfather.

Even though I resented the old man for the amount of guilt and pressure and recrimination he'd subjected my dad to, I suppose that the simple fact of spending the first twelve years of my life living in my grandfather's proximity had indelibly stamped a certain set of moral values and conditions upon me. I was never so extreme in my beliefs concerning God, the family, and the flag as my father's father was, but if I look at myself today I can see basic notions of decency that were passed down direct from him to me. His name was Hollis Wordsworth Mason, and perhaps because my parents had flattered the old man by naming me after him, he always took a special concern over my upbringing and moral instruction. One of the things that he took great pains to impress upon me was that country folk were morally healthier than city folk and that cities were just cesspools into which all the world's dishonesty and greed and lust and godlessness drained and was left to fester unhindered. Obviously, as I got older and came to realize just how much drunkenness and domestic violence and child abuse was hidden behind the neighborly facade of some of these lonely Montana farmhouses, I understood that my grandfather's appraisal had been a little one-sided. Nevertheless, some of the things that I saw in the city during my first few years here filled me with a sort of ethical revulsion that I couldn't shake off. To some degree, I still can't.

The pimps, the pornographers, the protection artists. The landlords who set dogs on their elderly tenants when they wanted them out to make way for more lucrative custom. The old men who touched little children and the callous young rapists who were barely old enough to shave. I saw these people all around me and I'd feel sick in my gut at the world and what it was becoming. Worse, there were times when I'd upset my dad and mom by loudly wishing I was back in Montana. Despite everything, I wished no such thing, but sometimes I'd be mad at them and it seemed like the best way to hurt them, to reawaken all those old doubts and worries and sleeping dogs of guilt. I'm sorry I did it now, and I wish I could have told them that while they were alive. I wish I could have told them that they were right in bringing me to the city, that they did the right thing by me. I wish I could have let them know that. Their lives would have been so much easier.

Masked adventurers make the front page. (New York Gazette, October 14th, 1938) Note artist's impression of "The Hooded Vigilante."

When the gap between the world of the city and the world my grandfather had presented to me as right and good became too wide and depressing to tolerate, I'd turn to my other great love, which was pulp adventure fiction. Despite the fact that Hollis Mason Senior would have had nothing but scorn and loathing for all of those violent and garish magazines, there was a sort of prevailing morality in them that I'm sure he would have responded to. The world of Doc Savage and The Shadow was one of absolute values, where what was good was never in the slightest doubt and where what was evil inevitably suffered some fitting punishment. The notion of good and justice espoused by Lamont Cranston with his slouch hat and blazing automatics seemed a long way from that of the fierce and taciturn old man I remembered sitting up alone into the Montana night with no company save his bible, but I can't help feeling that if the two had ever met they'd have found something to talk about. For my part, all those brilliant and resourceful sleuths and heroes offered a glimpse of a perfect world where morality worked the way it was *meant* to. Nobody in Doc Savage's world ever killed themselves except thwarted kamikaze assassins or enemy spies with cyanide capsules. Which world would you rather live in, if you had the choice?

Answering that question, I suppose, was what led me to become a cop. It was also what led me to later become something more than a cop. Bear that in mind and I think the rest of this narrative will be easier to swallow. I know people always have trouble understanding just what brings a person to behave the way that I and people like me behave, what makes us do the sort of things we do. I can't answer for anybody else, and I suspect that all our answers would be different anyway, but in my case it's fairly straightforward: I like the idea of adventure, and I feel bad unless I'm doing good. I've heard all the psychologists' theories, and I've heard all the jokes and the rumors and the innuendo, but what it comes down to for me is that I dressed up like an owl and fought crime because it was fun and because it needed doing and because I goddam felt like it.

Okay. There it is. I've said it. I dressed up. As an owl. And fought crime. Perhaps you begin to see why I half expect this summary of my career to raise more laughs than poor cuckolded Moe Vernon with his foam teats and his Wagner could ever hope to have done.

For me, it all started in 1938, the year when they invented the super-hero. I was too old for comic books when the first issue of ACTION COMICS came out, or at least too old to read them in public without souring my promotion chances, but I noticed a lot of the little kids on my beat reading it and couldn't resist asking one of them if I could glance through it. I figured if anybody saw me I could put it all down to keeping a good relationship with the youth of the community.

There was a lot of stuff in that first issue. There were detective yarns and stories about magicians whose names I can't remember, but from the moment I set eyes on it I only had eyes for the Superman story. Here was something that presented the basic morality of the pulps without all their darkness and ambiguity. The atmosphere of the horrific and faintly sinister that hung around the Shadow was nowhere to be seen in the bright primary colors of Superman's world, and there was no hint of the repressed sex-urge which had sometimes been apparent in the pulps, to my discomfort and embarrassment. I'd never been entirely sure what Lamont Cranston was up to with Margo Lane, but I'd bet it was nowhere near as innocent and wholesome as Clark Kent's relationship with her namesake Lois. Of course, all of these old characters are gone and forgotten now, but I'm willing to bet that there are at least a few older readers out there who will remember enough to know what I'm talking about. Anyway, suffice it to say that I read that story through about eight times before giving it back to the complaining kid that I'd snitched it from.

It set off a lot of things I'd forgotten about, deep inside me, and kicked all those old fantasies that I'd had when I was thirteen or fourteen back into gear: The prettiest girl in the class would be attacked by bullies, and I'd be there to beat them off, but when she offered to kiss me as a reward, I'd refuse. Gangsters would kidnap my math teacher, Miss Albertine, and I'd track them down and kill them one by one until she was free, and then she'd break off her engagement with my sarcastic English teacher, Mr. Richardson, because she'd fallen hopelessly in love with her grim-faced and silent fourteen-year-old savior. All of this stuff came flooding back as I stood there gawking at the hijacked comic book, and even though I laughed at myself for having entertained such transparent juvenile fantasies, I didn't laugh as hard as I might have done. Not half as hard as I'd laughed at Moe Vernon, for example.

Anyway, although I'd occasionally manage to trick some unsuspecting tyke into lending me his most recent issue of the funnybook in question and then spend the rest of the day leaping tall buildings inside my head, my fantasies were to remain as fantasies until I opened a newspaper in the autumn of that same year and found that the super-heroes had escaped from their four-color world and invaded the plain, factual black and white of the headlines.

The first news story was simple and unpresupposing enough, but it shared enough elements with those fictions that were closest to my heart to make me notice it and file it in my memory for future reference. It concerned an attempted assault and robbery that had taken place in Queens, New York. A man and his girlfriend, walking home after a night at the theater, had been set upon by a gang of three men armed with guns. After relieving the couple of their valuables, the gang has started to beat and physically abuse the young man while threatening to indecently assault his girlfriend. At this point, the crime had been interrupted by a figure "Who dropped into the alleyway from above with something over his face" and proceeded to disarm the three attackers before beating them with such severity that all three required hospital treatment and that one subsequently lost the use of both legs as a result of a spinal injury. The witnesses' recounting of the event was confused and contradictory, but there was still something in the story that gave me a tingle of recognition. And then, a week later, it happened again.

Reportage on this second instance was more detailed. A supermarket stick-up had been prevented thanks to the intervention of "A tall man, built like a wrestler, who wore a black hood and cape and also wore a noose around his neck." This extraordinary being had crashed in through the window of the supermarket while the robbery was in progress and attacked the man responsible with such intensity and savagery that those not disabled immediately were only too willing to drop their guns and surrender. Connecting this incidence of masked intervention with its predecessor, the papers ran the story under a headline that read simply "Hooded Justice." The first masked adventurer outside comic books had been given his name.

Reading and rereading that news item, I knew that I had to be the second. I'd found my vocation.

ABSENT FRIENDS

Y'KNOW, THAT MAKES JUST *THREE* OF US *MINUTEMEN* LEFT NOW. ME, *HOLLIS MASON*, AND POOR *BYRON LEWIS*, IN THE *BUGHOUSE* IN *MAINE*.

FUNNY... *EDDIE* WAS THE *YOUNGEST*. ALWAYS JOKIN' ABOUT HOW *OLD* WE ALL WERE.

"HE SAID HE'D *BURY* US.

"Y'SEE, THAT WAS *EDDIE*, ALWAYS TALKIN' LIKE HE WAS ON *TOP* OF IT, LIKE IT WAS NEVER GOING TO *HAPPEN* TO HIM..."

EDWARD MORGAN BLAKE
1924-1985

HE WAS *THE COMEDIAN*.

HE ALWAYS THOUGHT HE'D GET THE *LAST LAUGH.*

3

YEAH? WELL, JON TOLD ME ABOUT SOME OF THE STUFF BLAKE DID IN 'NAM. SOUNDS LIKE HE HAD A STRANGE SENSE OF HUMOR.

OH! SPEAKING OF WHICH, THAT REMINDS ME...

YOU REMEMBER THAT GUY WHO WRITES ME LETTERS? WELL, HE SENT ME AN ITEM OF MEMORABILIA...

THE ONE WHO ASKED FOR YOUR OLD COSTUME? HONESTLY, MOM, YOU ENCOURAGE THESE GUYS...

WHAT IS IT?

IT'S A TIJUANA BIBLE... A LITTLE EIGHT-PAGE PORNO COMIC THEY DID IN THE '30S AND '40S...

THEY DID 'EM ABOUT NEWSPAPER FUNNIES CHARACTERS LIKE BLONDIE, EVEN REAL PEOPLE LIKE MAE WEST.

THIS ONE'S ABOUT ME.

ABOUT...?

OH, GOD! MOTHER, THIS IS JUST GROSS! SOMEBODY SENT YOU THIS?

SURE. LISTEN, THOSE THINGS ARE VALUABLE, LIKE ANTIQUES. EIGHTY BUCKS AN' UP. I THINK IT'S KINDA FLATTERING.

FLATTERING...?

BEING REMINDED THAT PEOPLE USED TO SLOBBER OVER ME? SURE. FLATTERING. WHY NOT?

LAURIE, I'M 65. EVERY DAY THE FUTURE LOOKS A LITTLE BIT DARKER. BUT THE PAST, EVEN THE GRIMY PARTS OF IT...

...WELL, IT JUST KEEPS ON GETTING BRIGHTER ALL THE TIME.

OKAY, THAT'S IT! NICE PICTURE, FOLKS!

WE CAN MOVE? I CAN FINALLY SCRATCH MY ARMPIT?

OOOH! I GOT SPOTS IN MY EYES...

4

THE OTHERS ARE ALL WAITING TO ...

YOU VICIOUS LITTLE SON OF A BITCH...

HEY, WAIT! SHE WANTED ME TO DO IT! SHE...

NNNAH

YOU SICK LITTLE BASTARD, I'M GOING TO BREAK YOUR NECK...

UUUGGH

¿HUHH¿

¿AHUHH¿

THIS IS WHAT YOU LIKE, HUH?

THIS IS WHAT GETS YOU HOT...

GET OUT.

¿AHUHH¿ ¿HUHHH¿ OH, SURE. SURE. I'M GOING. BUT I GOT YOUR NUMBER, SEE? AND ONE OF THESE DAYS, THE JOKE'S GONNA BE ON YOU...

GET OUT!

7

AAAAAAAA

Panel 1: OH, GOD, PLEASE...

PLEASE, THIS MUST BE A MISTAKE! YOU HAVE THE WRONG PERSON...

NO.

EDGAR WILLIAM JACOBI, ALSO KNOWN AS EDGAR WILLIAM VAUGHN, ALSO KNOWN AS WILLIAM EDGAR BRIGHT...

...ALSO KNOWN AS MOLOCH.

Panel 3: I... I DON'T KNOW WHAT YOU'RE TALKING ABOUT. I'M A BUSINESSMAN, A RETIRED BUSINESSM--

AAAA!

LYING. DO IT AGAIN, BROKEN ARM. NOT JOKING.

Panel 4: OH, GOD, PLEASE ...I SPENT THE SEVENTIES IN JAIL. I'M NOT MOLOCH ANY-MORE. I JUST WANT TO BE LEFT ALONE. WHAT DO YOU WANT WITH ME?

HEARD YOU ATTENDED FUNERAL TODAY.

WHY?

Panel 5: THE FUNERAL?

I... I DON'T KNOW. I DON'T KNOW WHY I WENT.

I JUST FELT I SHOULD. I'D BEEN THINKING ABOUT THE COMEDIAN SINCE HE VISITED ME, AND...

Panel 6: AUHH! OH, GOD! WHAT DID I SAY?

HOW?

HOW DO YOU KNOW EDWARD BLAKE WAS THE COMEDIAN?

Panel 7: WH-WHEN HE BROKE IN, TO SEE ME! HE WAS DRUNK. HAD HIS MASK OFF. THE GUY WAS SCARED OF SOMETHING, CRYING...

ENEMIES FOR FORTY YEARS. WHY SHOULD HE VISIT YOU?

Panel 8: I DON'T KNOW. I WOKE UP, HE WAS THERE, IN MY ROOM, DRUNK, BABBLING, NOT MAKING SENSE...

I SAT IN BED, SCARED STIFF. HE SOUNDED CRAZY. I THOUGHT HE WAS GONNA KILL ME.

Panel 9: "THIS WAS, LIKE, A WEEK BEFORE I HEARD HE'D DIED.

"I GUESS IT WAS HIS LAST PERFORMANCE."

21

UNDER THE HOOD

III.

Presented here are the excerpts from UNDER THE HOOD. In these next chapters Hollis Mason discusses the formation of the Minutemen. Reprinted with permission of the author.

From the moment that I decided somewhere deep inside myself that I wanted to try my hand at being a costumed adventurer, to the moment I first stepped out into the night with a mask on my face and the wind on my bare legs, took about three months. Three months of self-doubt and self-ridicule. Three months of self-conscious training down at the Police Gymnasium. Three months figuring out how the hell I was going to make myself a costume.

The costume was difficult, because I couldn't start designing it until I'd thought of a name. This stumped me for a couple of weeks, because every name I came up with sounded stupid, and what I really wanted was something with the same sense of drama and excitement as "Hooded Justice."

Eventually, a suitable handle was provided inadvertently by one of the other cops that I worked with down at the station house. He'd invited me out for a beer after work two or three times only to be turned down because I wanted to spend as much of my evenings working out in the Police Gymnasiums as possible, after which I'd usually go to bed around nine o'clock and sleep through until five the next morning, when I'd get up and put in a couple of hours workout before donning my badge and uniform in readiness for my day job. After having his offer of beer and relaxation turned down yet again by reason of me wanting to be in bed early, he finally gave up asking and took to calling me "Nite Owl" out of sarcasm until he finally found somebody else to drink with.

"Nite Owl." I liked it. Now all I had to come up with was the costume.

A masked adventurer's costume is one of those things that nobody really thinks about. Should it have a cape, or no cape? Should it be thick and armored to protect you from harm, or flexible and lightweight to allow maneuverability? What sort of mask should it have? Do bright colors make you more of a target than dark ones? All of these were things that I had to consider.

Eventually, I opted for a design that left the arms and legs as free as possible, while protecting my body and head with a tough leather tunic, light chainmail briefs, and a layer of leather-over-chainmail protecting my head. I experimented with a cloak, remembering how the Shadow would use his cloak to misguide enemy bullets, leading them to shoot at parts of the swirling black mass where his body didn't happen to be. In practice, however, I found it too unwieldy. I was always tripping over it or getting it caught in things, and so I abandoned it for an outfit that was as streamlined as I could make it.

With the mail and leather headpiece hiding my hair, I found I only really needed a small domino mask to conceal my identity, but even this presented problems that weren't obvious at first glance. My first mask was attached to my face by the simple expediency of a string, but this nearly got me killed during my first ever outing in full costume, when a drunk with a knife hooked his fingers into the eyeholes of the domino and pulled it down so that I could only see out of one eye. If I'd been less fit and alert or he'd been less drunk my career might well have ended then. As it was I was able to tear off the mask completely and then disarm him, trusting that the alcohol would fog any clear recollection of my face. After that, I dispensed with the string and stuck the mask to my face using spirit gum, such as actors use to attach false beards or mustaches.

I first became Nite Owl during the early months of 1939, and although my first few exploits were largely unspectacular, they aroused a lot of media interest simply because by 1939, dressing up in costume and protecting your neighborhood had become something of a fad, with the whole of America at least briefly interested in its development. A month after I made my debut, a young woman who called herself The Silhouette broke into the headlines by exposing the activities of a crooked publisher trafficking in child pornography, delivering a punitive beating to the entrepreneur and his two chief cameramen in the process. A little after that, the first reports of a man dressed like a moth who could glide through the air started to come in from Connecticut, and a particularly vicious and brutal young man in a gaudy yellow boiler suit started cleaning up the city's waterfronts under the name of The Comedian. Within twelve months of Hooded Justice's dramatic entrance into the public consciousness, there were at least seven other costumed vigilantes operating on or around America's West Coast.

There was Captain Metropolis, who brought a knowledge of military technique and strategy to his attempt at eradicating organized crime in the inner urban areas, and who is still active to this day.

There was The Silk Spectre, now retired and living with her daughter after an unsuccessful early marriage, who in retrospect was probably the first of us ever to realize that there could be commercial benefits in being a masked adventurer. The Silk Spectre used her reputation as a crimefighter primarily to make the front pages and receive exposure for her lucrative modeling career, but I think all of us who knew her loved her a little bit and we certainly didn't begrudge her a living. I think we were all too unsure of our own motives to cast aspersions upon anybody else.

There was Dollar Bill, originally a star college athlete from Kansas who was actually employed as an in-house super-hero by one of the major national banks, when they realized that the masked man fad made being able to brag about having a hero of your own to protect your customer's money a very interesting publicity prospect. Dollar Bill was one of the nicest and most straightforward men I have ever met, and the fact that he died so tragically young is something that still upsets me whenever I think about it. While attempting to stop a raid upon one of his employer's banks, his cloak became entangled in the bank's revolving door and he was shot dead at point-blank range before he could free it. Designers employed by the bank had designed his costume for maximum publicity appeal. If he'd designed it himself he might have left out that damned stupid cloak and still be alive today.

There was Mothman and The Silhouette and The Comedian and there was me, all of us choosing to dress up in gaudy opera costumes and express the notion of good and evil in simple, childish terms, while over in Europe they were turning human beings into soap and lampshades. We were sometimes respected, sometimes analyzed, and most often laughed at, and in spite of all the musings above, I don't think that those of us still surviving today are any closer to understanding just why we *really* did it all. Some of us did it because we were hired to and some of us did it to gain publicity. Some of us did it out of a sense of childish excitement and some of us, I think, did it for a kind of excitement that was altogether more adult if perhaps less healthy. They've called us fascists and they've called us perverts and while there's an element of truth in both those accusations, neither of them are big enough to take in the whole picture.

Yes, some of us were politically extreme. Before Pearl Harbor, I heard Hooded Justice openly expressing approval for the activities of Hitler's Third Reich, and Captain Metropolis has gone on record as making statements about black and Hispanic Americans that have been viewed as both racially prejudiced and inflammatory, charges that it is difficult to argue or deny.

Yes, I daresay some of us did have our sexual hang-ups. Everybody knows what eventually became of the Silhouette and although it would be tasteless to rehash the events surrounding her death in this current volume, it provides proof for those who need it that for some people, dressing up in a costume did have its more libidinous elements.

Yes, some of us were unstable and neurotic. Only a week ago as of this writing, I received word that the man behind the mask and wings of Mothman, whose true identity I am not at liberty to divulge, has been committed to a mental institution after a long bout of alcoholism and a complete mental breakdown.

Yes, we were crazy, we were kinky, we were Nazis, all those things that people say. We were also doing something because we believed in it. We were attempting, through our personal efforts, to make our country a safer and better place to live in. Individually, working on our separate patches of turf, we did too much good in our respective communities to be written off as mere aberration, whether social or sexual or psychological.

It was only when we got together that the problems really started. I sometimes think without the Minutemen we might all have given up and called it quits pretty soon. The costumed adventurer might have become quietly and simply extinct.

And the world might not be in the mess it's in today.

IV.

There's no mystery behind how the Minutemen first got together. Captain Metropolis had written to Sally Jupiter care of her agent, suggesting that they might meet with a view to forming a group of masked adventurers who could pool their resources and experience to combat crime. The Captain has always had a strategic approach to crimefighting, so I can see why the idea would appeal to him, although back then I was surprised that he'd made an effort to get in touch with Sally. He was so polite and reserved that Sally's drinking, swearing and mode of dress were guaranteed to shock him speechless. Later, I realized that Sally was simply the only costumed vigilante forethoughtful enough to have an agent whose address was in the phone book.

Sally's agent (and, much later, her husband) was an extremely shrewd individual named Laurence Schexnayder. He realized that without the occasional gimmick to revitalize flagging public interest, the fad for long underwear heroes would eventually fade, reducing his girl Sally's chances of media exposure as The Silk Spectre to zero. Thus it was Schexnayder, in mid-1939, who suggested placing a large ad in the Gazette asking other mystery men to come forward.

One by one we came, over the next few weeks. We were introduced to Sally, to Captain Metropolis, to each other and to Laurence Schexnayder. He was very organized and professional, and although only in his mid-thirties he seemed very mature and respectable to us back then. Maybe that was just because he'd be the only person in the room not wearing their boxer shorts over their pants. By the fall of '39 he'd arranged all the publicity and the Minutemen were finally born.

The *real* mystery is how the hell we managed to *stay* together.

Dressing up in a costume takes a very extreme personality, and the chances of eight such personalities getting along together were about seventy-eleven million to one against. This isn't to say that some of us didn't get along, of course. Sally attached herself pretty swiftly to Hooded Justice, who was one of the biggest men I've ever seen. I never found out his real name, but I'd be willing to bet that those early news reports weren't far off in comparing him to a wrestler. Strangely enough, even though Sally would always be hanging onto his arm, he never seemed very interested in *her*. I don't think I ever saw him kiss her, although maybe that was just because of his mask. Anyway, they started going out together, sort of, after the first Minutemen Christmas Party in 1939, which is the last time I can remember us all having a real good time together. After that, things went bad. We had worms in the apple, eating it from inside.

The first Minutemen Christmas party, 1939
(from left to right) The Silhouette, Silk Spectre,
Comedian, Hooded Justice, Captain Metropolis
(in mirror), Nite Owl, Mothman, Dollar Bill

The worst of these was the Comedian. I'm aware that he's still active today and even respected in some quarters, but I know what I know, and that man is a disgrace to our profession. In 1940 he attempted to sexually assault Sally Jupiter in the Minutemen trophy room after a meeting. He left the group shortly thereafter by mutual consent and with a minimum of publicity. Schexnayder had persuaded Sally not to press charges against the Comedian for the good of the group's image, and she complied. The Comedian went his way unscathed…even though he was badly wounded in an unconnected stabbing incident about a year later. This is what made him decide to change his flimsy yellow costume for the leather armor he wears at present. He went on to make a name for himself as a

Newsreel footage of the Comedian in the South Pacific, 1942

war hero in the Pacific, but all I can think of is the bruises along Sally Jupiter's ribcage and hope to God that America can find itself a better class of hero than *that*.

After that, things deteriorated. In 1946, the papers revealed that the Silhouette was living with another woman in a lesbian relationship. Schexnayder persuaded us to expel her from the group, and six weeks later she was murdered, along with her lover, by one of her former enemies. Dollar Bill was shot dead, and in 1947 the group was dealt its most serious blow when

Early publicity poster of Moloch, 1937

Sally quit crimefighting to marry her agent. We always thought she might come back, but in 1949 she had a daughter, so that clinched that. Eventually, those of us who were left didn't even fight crime anymore. It wasn't interesting. The villains we'd fought with were either in prison or had moved on to less glamorous activities. Moloch, for example, who had started out aged seventeen as a stage magician, evolving into an ingenious and flamboyant criminal mastermind through underworld contacts made in his world of nightclubs, had moved into impersonal crime like drugs, financial fraud and vice clubs by the late '40s. Eventually, there was just me, Mothman, Hooded Justice and Captain Metropolis sitting around in a meeting hall that smelled like a locker room now that there weren't any women in the group. There was nobody interesting left to fight, nothing notable to talk about. In 1949, we called it a day. By then, however, we'd been around long enough to somehow inspire younger people, God help them, to follow in our footsteps.

The Minutemen were finished, but it didn't matter. The damage had already been done.

THE JUDGE OF ALL THE EARTH

HE COULDN'T *RELATE* TO ME. NOT *EMOTIONALLY.* CERTAINLY NOT *SEXUALLY.*

WITHIN *THREE YEARS* HE'D *DUMPED* ME FOR SOME *SIXTEEN-YEAR-OLD* WHO RAN AROUND IN HER *UNDERWEAR.*

"ONE DAY, HE'LL FIND OUT. HE'LL FIND OUT WHAT IT *FEELS* LIKE."

SPECIAL TALENT QUARTERS

VISITORS ENTRANCE

" I SEE. SO, MS. *SLATER,* HOW DO *YOU* FEEL, NOW THAT YOU'VE LEARNED ABOUT YOUR *CONDITION?* "

BITTER. BITTER AS *HELL.* I STARTED *SMOKING...* THREE PACKS A *DAY,* I FIGURE, "WHY NOT?"

I MEAN, I HAVE NO *ILLUSIONS...*

"I MEAN, NOBODY'S GONNA *MISS* ME! AFTER I'M *GONE,* NOBODY'S GONNA MISS ME. I KNOW *THAT.*

"ESPECIALLY NOT *HIM.*"

ROCKEFELLER MILITARY RESEARCH CENTER

TAX

OFF

Y'SEE, HE DOESN'T *CARE!* HE DOESN'T HAVE TO GET *OLD!* THAT'S... ⸮AHH-HUH⸮ EXCUSE ME...

THAT'S WHY I'M TALKING TO *YOU* PEOPLE. I WANT THE *WORLD* TO KNOW ABOUT HIM, WHAT HE *DID* TO ME...

"I KEPT *QUIET* ALL THESE *YEARS,* BUT THEN THIS *LATEST* THING HAPPENED AND I HAD TO LET IT ALL *OUT*...

"⸮AHHUK⸮

"EXCUSE ME."

6

OH! SO, DR. OSTERMAN FINALLY ARRIVES AND NOBODY THINKS TO TELL ME! MARVELOUS!

DUH--DON'T BLAME ME! I ONLY JUST TOOK OVER RECEPTION AN' HE JUST APPEARED!

I FEEL SICK. THEY'RE NOT PAYING ME ENOUGH FOR THIS...

"THEY'RE NOT PAYING ME ENOUGH TO HANDLE MONSTERS FROM OUTTA SPACE!"

CINEMA
IS ISLAND EARTH

YOU HAVEN'T LEFT US TIME FOR MAKEUP! THAT BLUE IS FAR TOO LIGHT FOR TELEVISION...

DR. OSTERMAN? I'M FORBES, ARMY INTELLIGENCE. HERE'S A LIST OF NO-GO AREAS. OBVIOUSLY, AFGHANISTAN WILL ARISE, BUT PLAY IT COOL...

"...AND TRY NOT TO GET INTO ANY TIGHT CORNERS."

IS THIS DARK ENOUGH?

MY GOD.

UHH, WELL, YES. YES, THAT'S JUST PERFECT...

"THAT'S CERTAINLY DARK ENOUGH FOR MY PURPOSES."

11

AS FAR AS I KNOW, THERE IS NO SITUATION IN AFGHANISTAN CURRENTLY REQUIRING MY *ATTENTIONS.*

OKAY, FINE. NOW HOW ABOUT YOU OVER *THERE.* YES, *YOU, SIR.* AND *PLEASE...*

" *LET'S TRY AND KEEP IT SNAPPY.* "

DR. OSTERMAN, I'M *DOUG ROTH,* I WRITE FOR *NOVA EXPRESS.*

I WONDER IF YOU REMEMBER *WALLY WEAVER.* BACK IN THE EARLY *SIXTIES,* THE NEWSPAPERS CALLED HIM *"DR. MANHATTAN'S BUDDY."*

HE *DIED* OF *CANCER* IN 1971.

" *I BELIEVE IT WAS QUITE SUDDEN AND QUITE PAINFUL.* "

I REMEMBER WALLY AS A GOOD *FRIEND.* I ATTENDED HIS *FUNERAL.*

HOW ABOUT *EDGAR W. JACOBI,* ALSO KNOWN AS *MOLOCH?* YOU ENCOUNTERED *HIM SEVERAL* TIMES DURING THE SIXTIES IN *BATTLES, CONFLICTS...*

REALLY?

" *...WHATEVER IT IS YOU SUPER-PEOPLE DO.* "

13

DR. MANHATTAN, HOW *OFTEN* DID...

I SAID LEAVE ME *ALONE!*

UH...WELL...

I GUESS I OUGHTTA GO FIND A *HOTEL.* I'M A BIT *WIPED OUT.* I MEAN, AFTER *THAT*... I MEAN, *JESUS,* *US!* GETTING *MUGGED!*

LOOK... I'M *SHAKING.* ONCE THE ADRENALINE WEARS OFF I *ALWAYS* FEEL SORTA *WEIRD*...

"SORTA *EMPTY.*"

WELL, LOOK, ARE YOU *SURE?* WHY NOT VISIT *HOLLIS* AND GET YOUR *BREATH* BACK?

UH-UH. I'VE HAD *ENOUGH* SUPER-HERO STUFF FOR ONE DAY.

I'M GONNA FIND A *HOTEL* AND THINK MY *RELATIONSHIP* OVER...

"...SEE IF I CAN COME UP WITH ONE GOOD REASON TO STICK *AROUND.*"

"GOD, Y'KNOW, IT FEELS SO MUCH *BETTER* NOW IT'S OUT IN THE *OPEN.* THANKS FOR *LISTENING.*"

ANYWAY, YOU TAKE *CARE* OF YOURSELF, DAN. IT'S A TOUGH *WORLD* OUT THERE.

YEAH. YOU *TOO,* LAURIE.

'BYE.

16

DANNY! HOW **ARE** YA?

YOU'RE **LATE.** I THOUGHT YOU'D HAD AN **ACCIDENT!**

NO... NO, I JUST HAD A LITTLE **SKIRMISH**...

YOU'RE NOT THE **ONLY** ONE. I JUST BEEN WATCHIN' **DOC MANHATTAN** ON T.V.! THEY JUST ABOUT **CRUCIFIED** THE POOR GUY...

JON? UH...

WHAT DO YOU **MEAN?**

SOME GUY STOOD UP AN' ACCUSED HIM OF GIVING A LOT OF PEOPLE **CANCER,** INCLUDING **JANEY SLATER.**

DOC LOOKED REAL **SHAKEN,** STARTED SHOUTING TO BE LEFT **ALONE.** ONE MOMENT, THE CAMERAS WERE IN **CLOSE** ON HIM...

... THE **NEXT,** THE SCREEN WENT **BLOOEY** AND THEN WE WERE GETTIN' PICTURES OF A **PARKING LOT.**

HE'D TELEPORTED EVERYBODY OUTTA THE **T.V. BUILDING,** CAMERAS AN' ALL.

BUT... BUT I WAS JUST WITH **LAURIE**. SHE DOESN'T **KNOW**...

WELL, SHE'LL KNOW SOON **ENOUGH.** THAT SHOW WENT OUT ON **PRIME TIME.**

THE WHOLE **WORLD** WILL KNOW SOON ENOUGH.

EDITED REPLAY

17

HA! I KNEW IT! WILLYA LOOKIT *THAT!*

SORRY THEY'RE *LATE.* THEY WANTED TO *WAIT* 'TIL THE *T.V. SHOW* WAS ON THE *AIR* BEFORE THEY PLAYED THE *GRAND SLAM.*

WE'D BEEN BLASTED TO FRAGMENTS BEFORE WE COULD WARN *DAVIDSTOWN* OF THE *HELL-SHIP'S* APPROACH. I ALONE SURVIVED UPON MY REMOTE *ATOLL.*

CANCER! I MIGHTA KNOWN! THEY OUGHTTA *DEPORT* THE RADIO-ACTIVE *GOON!* PUT HIM IN *EXILE!*

THE FREIGHTER'S MURDEROUS ONSLAUGHT HAD SURPRISED US.

HA! INSIDE, HIS *EX* SAYS THEY COULDN'T RELATE *SEXUALLY!* *THAT* MEANS HE'S QUEER AS A THREE-DOLLAR *BILL!*

MY *WIFE,* SHE'D *FANTASIZE* ABOUT THIS *CREEP! I* SUSPECTED ALL ALONG...

I THOUGHT OF MY *FAMILY: VULNERABLE, UNSUSPECTING...*

... NEVER DREAMING THAT *DAMNATION* BORE DOWN UPON THEM, SAILS PREGNANT WITH A *PIRATE WIND,* A NECKLACE OF *HEADS* ABOUT ITS *PROW.*

CRAZED WITH *HELPLESSNESS,* I CURSED *GOD* AND WEPT, WONDERING IF *HE* WEPT ALSO

BUT THEN, WHAT USE HIS *TEARS,* IF HIS *HELP* WAS DENIED ME?

HEY. IT'S *RAININ'.* LEND ME YOUR *CAP,* MAN, I'M GETTIN' *WET.*

NO CHANCE. I DON'T *LEND* THINGS. IT'S MY *PHILOSOPHY.*

SUIT Y'SELF, JIVE-ASS.

IN *THIS* WORLD, YOU SHOULDN'T RELY ON HELP FROM *ANYBODY.* IN THE *END,* A MAN STANDS *ALONE.*

MY OWN SOBBING HAD FRIGHTENED THE GULLS. THEY DEPARTED...

FALLOUT SHELTER

... AND IN THE TERRIBLE *SILENCE* I UNDERSTOOD THE TRUE BREADTH OF THE WORD "*ISOLATION.*"

SHELTER

ALL ALONE.

INNA *FINAL* ANALYSIS.

18

At play amidst the
Strangeness and Charm.

play amidst the
geness and Charm.

20

THAT NIGHT, I SLEPT BADLY BENEATH COLD, DISTANT STARS, PONDERING UPON THE COLD, DISTANT GOD IN WHOSE HANDS THE FATE OF DAVIDSTOWN RESTED.

WAS HE REALLY THERE?

HAD HE BEEN THERE ONCE, BUT NOW DEPARTED?

"...AND WE'RE ALL IN BIG TROUBLE!"

WMUH?

≈FNFF≈

≈FNFF-FNFF≈

GOOD MORNING, DANIEL.

BROUGHT YOU YOUR SUNDAY PAPER.

THE COMEDIAN MURDERED, DR. MANHATTAN EXILED...

TWO OF US GONE. ALL WITHIN A WEEK.

WHO NEXT? VEIDT? JUSPECZYK? ME?

YOU?

BY THE WAY, YOU NEED A STRONGER LOCK. THAT NEW ONE BROKE AFTER ONE SHOVE.

MY NEW LOCK?

POOR CHOICE. GET MORE EXPENSIVE ONE. CAN'T BE TOO SECURITY CONSCIOUS.

ESPECIALLY NOT THESE DAYS.

THESE DAYS, NOBODY'S SAFE.

BE SEEING YOU. THANKS FOR THE COFFEE AND CEREAL.

SUNDAY SECTIONS New York Gazette

DR. MANHATTA LEAVES EARTH

BENNY ANGER

24

25

Shall not the Judge of all the earth do right?   —GENESIS chapter 18, verse 25

UNDER THE HOOD

Presented here are the excerpts from UNDER THE HOOD. In this next chapter Hollis Mason discusses the traumas of the 1950s and the emergence of the new super-heroes. Reprinted with permission of the author.

V.

The Minutemen didn't get to usher in the 1950s with a Christmas celebration the way we'd ushered in the '40s, and perhaps that's appropriate. The decade following the disbanding of the group was cold and bleak, both for me in particular and for masked adventurers in general. Plus, it seemed to go on forever.

I think the worst thing was the belated realization of just how much a fad we'd always been, something to fill the dead columns of the newspapers right alongside the Hula Hoop and the Jitterbug. Ever since Sally Jupiter married her manager, his tireless, shrewd efforts as a publicist had been noticeably absent. He'd recognized that the day of the costumed hero was over – even though we hadn't – and he'd gotten out while the getting was good. Consequently, we found our exploits being reported less and less frequently. When they were reported, the tone

1947: Sally Jupiter marries Laurence Schexnayder. Can you spot the famous faces in the crowd?

was often derisive. I can remember a lot of hooded vigilante jokes coming into circulation during the early fifties. The mildest was one that suggested we were called The Minutemen due to our performance in the bedroom. There were an awful lot of bright blue gags about Sally Jupiter. I know, because she told me most of them herself the last time I saw her.

Sally had a baby girl named Laurel Jane in 1949, and it seemed to be right about then that her marital problems started. These were widely discussed, so I don't think I need repeat them here. Suffice it to say that the marriage ended in 1956, and since then Sally has done a first rate job of bringing her daughter up into a bright, spunky youngster that any mother could be proud of.

The thing about that particular decade is that things first started getting *serious* then. I remember thinking at the time that it was funny how the more serious things got, the better the Comedian seemed to do. Out of the whole bunch of us, he was the only one who was still right up there on the front pages, still making the occasional headline. On the strength of his military work he had good government connections, and it often seemed as if he was being groomed into some sort of patriotic symbol. At the height of the McCarthy era, nobody had any doubts about where the Comedian's feet were planted politically.

That was more than could be said for the rest of us. We all had to testify before the House UnAmerican Activities Committee, and were all forced to reveal our true identities to one of its representatives. Galling though this was, it didn't present any immediate problems for most of us. With Captain Metropolis having such an outstanding military record and with my own service in the police force, we both were more or less cleared of suspicion right away. Mothman met with more difficulty, mostly because of some left-wing friends he'd cultivated during his student days. He was eventually cleared, but the investigations were both lengthy and ruthless, and I think that the pressure he was under at that time prompted the beginnings of the drinking problem that has contributed so much to his later mental ill-health.

Only Hooded Justice refused to testify, on the grounds that he was not prepared to reveal

his true identity to anyone. When
pressed, he simply vanished . . . or at
least that's how it seemed. Vanishing is
no big problem when you're a
costumed hero – you just take your
costume off. It seemed quite likely that
Hooded Justice had simply chosen to
retire rather than reveal his identity,
which the authorities seemed perfectly
happy with.

The only detail concerning the
disappearance of America's first
masked adventurer that still nags at me
was trivial, and maybe not even
connected at all; it was brought up in
an article that appeared in *The New
Frontiersman,* almost a year after
Hooded Justice vanished. The author
mentioned the disappearance of a well
known circus strongman of the day
named Rolf Müller, who had quit his
job at the height of the Senate
Subcommittee hearings. Three
months later, a badly decomposed
body that was tentatively identified as
Müller's was pulled from the sea after
being washed up on the coast of
Boston. Müller, assuming the body
actually was that of the renowned

*(left) Hooded Justice (right) Rolf Müller.
Were they the same man?*

weightlifter, had been shot through the head. The inference of the article was that Müller,
whose family was East German, had gone on the run for fear of being uncovered while the
Communist witch hunts were at their most feverish. The piece also implied that Müller had
probably been executed by his own Red superiors.

I always wondered about that. Müller disappeared at almost exactly the same time as
Hooded Justice was last seen, and the two men had corresponding builds. Whether the body
washed up on that Boston shoreline belonged to Müller or not, neither he nor Hooded Justice
were ever seen or heard from again. Were they the same man? If they were, were they really
dead? If they were dead, who killed them? Was Hooded Justice really working for the Reds? I
don't know. Real life is messy, inconsistent, and it's seldom when anything ever really gets
resolved. It's taken me a long time to realize that.

One of the big problems that faced costumed heroes at the time was the absence of
costumed criminals of any real note. I don't think any of us realized how much we needed
those goons until they started to thin out. You see, if you're the only one who'd bothered to
turn up for a free-for-all in costume, you tended to look kind of stupid. If the bad guys joined
in as well, it wasn't so bad, but without them it was always sort of embarrassing. There had
never been as many costumed criminals as heroes, but with the end of the 1940s the trend
grew much more pronounced.

Most of the crooks turned in their costumes along with their criminal careers, but some
just opted for a less extroverted and more profitable approach. The new breed of villains,
despite their often colorful names, were mostly ordinary men in business suits who ran drug
and prostitution rackets. That's not to say they didn't cause as much trouble . . . far from it; I

just mean that they weren't as much fun to fight. All the cases I ended up investigating during the '50s seemed sordid and depressing and quite often blood-chillingly horrible. I don't know what it was...there just seemed to be a sort of bleak, uneasy feeling in the air. It was as if some essential element of our lives, of all our lives, was vanishing before we knew entirely what it was. I don't think I could really describe it completely except maybe to somebody who remembered the terrific elation we all felt after the war: we felt that we'd taken the worst that the 20th century could throw at us and stood our ground. We felt as if we'd really won a hard-earned age of peace and prosperity that would see us well into the year 2000. This optimism lasted all through the '40s and the early '50s, but by the middle of that latter decade it was starting to wear thin, and there was a sort of ominous feeling in the air.

Partly it was the beatniks, the jazz musicians and the poets openly condemning American values whenever they opened their mouths. Partly it was Elvis Presley and the whole Rock 'n' Roll boom. Had we fought a war for our country so that our daughters could scream and swoon over young men who looked like *this*, who sounded like *that*? With all these sudden social upheavals just when we thought we'd gotten everything straight, it was impossible to live through the 1950s without a sense of impending catastrophe bearing implacably down upon the whole country, the whole world. Some people thought it was war and others thought it was flying saucers, but those things weren't really what was bearing down upon us. What was bearing down upon us was the 1960s.

The '60s, along with the mini-skirt and the Beatles, brought one thing to the world that was significant above all others – its name was Dr. Manhattan. The arrival of Dr. Manhattan would make the terms "masked hero" and "costumed adventurer" as obsolete as the persons they described. A new phrase had entered the American language, just as a new and almost terrifying concept had entered its consciousness. It was the dawn of the Super-Hero.

Manhattan's existence was announced to the world in the March of 1960, and I don't think there can have been anybody on the planet who didn't feel that same strange jumble of emotions when they heard the news. Foremost amongst this assortment of sensations was disbelief. The idea of a being who could walk through walls, move from one place to another without covering the intervening distance and re-arrange things completely with a single thought was flat-out impossible. On the other hand, the people presenting this news to us were our own government. The notion that they might simply have made it up was equally improbable, and in the face of this contradiction, it became gradually easier to accept the dream-like unreality of those first newsreel images: a blue man melting a tank with a wave of his hand; the fragments of a disassembled rifle floating there eerily in the air with nobody touching them. Once accepted as reality, however, such things became no easier to digest. If you accept that floating rifle parts are real you also have to somehow accept that everything you've ever known to be a fact is probably untrue. That peculiar unease is something that most of us have learned to live with over the years, but it's still there.

The other emotions that accompanied the announcement were perhaps harder to identify and pin down. There was a certain elation...it felt as if Santa Claus had suddenly turned out to be real after all. Coupled with and complementary to this was a terrible and uneven sense of fear and uncertainty. While this was hard to define precisely, if I had to boil it down into three words, those words would be, "We've been replaced." I'm not just talking about the non-powered costumed hero fraternity here, you understand, although Dr. Manhattan's appearance was certainly one of the factors that led to my own increased feelings of obsolescence and my eventual decision to quit the hero business altogether. You see, while masked vigilantes had certainly been made obsolete, so in a sense had every other living organism upon the planet. I don't think that society has fully realized yet just exactly what Dr. Manhattan's arrival means; how much it's likely to change every detail of our lives.

Although Dr. Manhattan was the most prominent by far of the 'New Breed' of costumed heroes, he wasn't quite the first nor by any means the last. In the closing months of 1958, the papers mentioned that a major opium and heroin smuggling racket had been busted by a young adventurer named Ozymandias, who seemed to have quickly gained a reputation amongst the criminal fraternity for his boundless and implacable intelligence, not to mention a large degree of athletic prowess.

I met both Dr. Manhattan and Ozymandias for the first time at a charity event in the June of 1960. Ozymandias seemed to be a nice young fellow, although I personally found Dr. Manhattan to be a little distant. Maybe that was more my fault than his, though, since I found it very difficult to feel easy around the guy, even once I'd got used to the shock of his physical presence. It's a strange feeling…the first time you meet him your brain wants to scream, blow a fuse and shut itself down immediately, refusing to accept that he exists. This lasts for a couple of minutes, at which time he's still there and hasn't gone away, and in the end you just accept him because he's standing there and talking to you and after a while it almost seems normal.

Almost.

Anyway, at that charity event…I think it was Red Cross relief for the ongoing famine in India…a lot of things became apparent to me. Looking around at the other adventurers there, I wasn't happy with what I saw: The Comedian was there, imposing his overbearing personality and his obnoxious cigar smoke upon anyone within reach. Mothman was there, a glass in one hand, slurring his words and letting his sentences trail off into incoherence. Captain Metropolis was there, his paunch starting to show despite a strict regimen of Canadian Air Force Exercises. Finally, leaving the two younger heroes aside for a moment, there was me: Forty-six years old and starting to feel it, still trying to cut it in the company of guys who could level a mountain by snapping their fingers. I think it was when that moment of self insight hit me that I first decided to finally hang up my mask and get myself a proper job. I'd been about due to retire from the police force for some time, and I started wondering about what I wanted to do now that the thrill of adventure had finally started to pale. Looking back over my life, I tried to work out what I'd been doing during my existence's happier stretches, in order to form a basis for my future contentment.

After much deliberation, I concluded that I'd never been happier than when helping my dad beat some sense into an obstinate engine down at Moe Vernon's yard. After a life of crime-fighting, no notion seemed sweeter to me than that of spending my autumn years contentedly making dead vehicles run again in the confines of my own auto repair shop.

In the May of this year, 1962, that's exactly what I opted to do.

I retired. To mend cars. Probably for the rest of my life. As I see it, part of the art of being a hero is knowing when you don't need to be one anymore, realizing that the game has changed and that the stakes are different and that there isn't necessarily a place for you in this strange new pantheon of extraordinary people. The world has moved on, and I'm content to watch it from my armchair with a beer by my side and the smell of fresh oil still on my fingers.

Part of my contentment comes from knowing that there have maybe been some overall consequence of my twenty-three years behind the mask. This knowledge came to me in the shape of a letter from a young man whose name I'm not at liberty to reveal. He told me of his great admiration for my efforts as Nite Owl and proposed that since I'd retired and would no longer be using the name, perhaps he could borrow it since he intended to follow my example and become a crime-fighter. I've visited his home since then and seen some of the fabulous technology he intends to bring to bear on the war against crime. I was certainly far too impressed to refuse him the use of what I'd always thought was dumb name to begin with, so by the time this sees print there may well be a new Nite Owl patrolling the streets of New York. Also, Sally Jupiter tells me that as soon as little Laurie's old enough she wants to be a super-heroine just like her mom, so who knows? It seems as if from being a novelty nine-day wonder, the super-hero has become a part of American life. It's here to stay.

For better, or for worse.

THE PHOTOGRAPH IS IN MY HAND.

IT IS THE PHOTOGRAPH OF A MAN AND A WOMAN. THEY ARE AT AN AMUSEMENT PARK, IN 1959.

IN TWELVE SECONDS TIME, I DROP THE PHOTOGRAPH TO THE SAND AT MY FEET, WALKING AWAY. IT'S ALREADY LYING THERE, TWELVE SECONDS INTO THE FUTURE.

TEN SECONDS NOW.

THE PHOTOGRAPH IS IN MY HAND.

I FOUND IT IN A DERELICT BAR AT THE GILA FLATS TEST BASE, TWENTY-SEVEN HOURS AGO.

IT'S STILL THERE, TWENTY-SEVEN HOURS INTO THE PAST, IN ITS FRAME, IN THE DARKENED BAR.

I'M STILL THERE, LOOKING AT IT.

THE PHOTOGRAPH IS IN MY HAND. THE WOMAN TAKES A PIECE OF POPCORN BETWEEN THUMB AND FOREFINGER. THE FERRIS WHEEL PAUSES.

SEVEN SECONDS NOW.

IT'S OCTOBER, 1985. I'M ON MARS. IT'S JULY, 1959. I'M IN NEW JERSEY, AT THE PAL-ISADES AMUSEMENT PARK.

FOUR SECONDS. THREE.

I'M TIRED OF LOOKING AT THE PHOTOGRAPH NOW.

I OPEN MY FINGERS. IT FALLS TO THE SAND AT MY FEET.

I AM GOING TO LOOK AT THE STARS.

THEY ARE SO FAR AWAY, AND THEIR LIGHT TAKES SO LONG TO REACH US...

ALL WE EVER SEE OF STARS ARE THEIR OLD PHOTOGRAPHS.

IT'S RIGHT THROUGH HERE...

WALLY STEERS ME FROM THE ARIZONA SUNLIGHT INTO THE CROWDED BAR. THERE'S A SUDDEN SENSATION OF *DÉJÀ VU*: I'VE SEEN THIS PLACE *BEFORE*...

... EXCEPT THAT IT WAS *DESERTED* THEN, DERELICT, WITH STARLIGHT SHINING DOWN UPON ITS ROTTED FLOORBOARDS, THROUGH THE COLLAPSED CEILING...

THE ILLUSION VANISHES, ALMOST BEFORE IT HAS REGISTERED. IT'S MAY 12TH, 1959. WALLY IS INTRODUCING ME TO SOMEONE...

JANEY SLATER, MEET JON OSTERMAN. JON'S FROM *PRINCETON*.

OHHH... THE *NEW* GUY! YOU'RE REPLACING *HANK MEADOWS*, RIGHT?

I AM?

I *GUESS* SO. HANK DIED LAST *FALL*, SOME KINDA *TUMOR*. THERE'S HIS *PICTURE* BEHIND THE *BAR* THERE. THE GUY WITH *GLASSES*.

Y'KNOW, YOU'RE PRETTY *YOUNG* FOR A *RESEARCH SCIENTIST*.

WELL, YOU KNOW... MY *DAD* SORT OF *PUSHED* ME INTO IT. THAT HAPPENS TO ME A *LOT*. OTHER PEOPLE SEEM TO MAKE ALL MY MOVES *FOR* ME.

MM. I'LL BET.

CAN I GET YOU A *DRINK*?

SHE BUYS ME A BEER, THE FIRST TIME A WOMAN HAS EVER DONE THIS FOR ME. AS SHE PASSES ME THE COLD, PERSPIRING GLASS, OUR FINGERS TOUCH...

IT'S 1963. WE'RE MAKING LOVE AFTER AN *ARGUMENT*, OUR *TENDERNESS* IN DIRECT PROPORTION TO ITS *VIOLENCE*...

IT'S 1966, AND SHE'S *PACKING*: TEARFUL, CARELESS WITH ANGER...

THE PHOTOGRAPH LIES IN THE SAND AT MY FEET.

5

IT'S OCTOBER, 1985. I'M BASKING IN THE TWO-MILLION-YEAR-OLD LIGHT OF ANDROMEDA. I CAN SEE THE SUPERNOVA THAT ERNST HARTWIG DISCOVERED IN 1885, A CENTURY AGO.

IT SCINTILLATES, A WINK INTENDED FOR THE TRILOBITES, ALL LONG DEAD.

SUPERNOVAS ARE WHERE GOLD FORMS; THE ONLY PLACE. ALL GOLD COMES FROM SUPERNOVAS.

IT'S CHRISTMAS, 1959...

DO...DO YOU LIKE IT? I MEAN, IS THAT THE SORT OF THING THAT YOU LIKE, NOW THAT YOU'RE, UH...

YOU KNOW.

I LIKE IT VERY MUCH. ITS ATOMIC STRUCTURE IS A PERFECT GRID, LIKE A CHECKERBOARD. IT'S...

JANEY? WHAT'S UP? ARE YOU COLD? I CAN RAISE THE TEMPERATURE...

NO...I'M NOT COLD.

I'M SCARED.

OF ME?

NO. YES. OH, GOD, LOOK, I...

I'M JUST SCARED BECAUSE EVERYTHING FEELS WEIRD. IT'S AS IF EVERYTHING'S CHANGED. NOT JUST YOU: EVERYTHING!

I MEAN, I DON'T KNOW WHAT YOU ARE. NOBODY DOES. YOU WERE DISINTEGRATED, YOU PUT YOURSELF BACK TOGETHER...

THEY SAY YOU CAN DO ANYTHING, JON. THEY SAY YOU'RE LIKE GOD NOW.

I DON'T THINK THERE IS A GOD, JANEY. IF THERE IS, I'M NOT HIM.

I'M STILL THE SAME PERSON. NOTHING'S CHANGED. I STILL WANT YOU...

I'LL ALWAYS WANT YOU.

AS I LIE I HEAR HER SHOUTING AT ME IN 1963; SOBBING IN 1966. MY FINGERS OPEN. THE PHOTOGRAPH IS FALLING...

11

NOW IT'S *JUNE*, A CHARITY EVENT WITH SEVERAL COSTUMED ADVENTURERS ATTENDING ...FRIENDLY MIDDLE-AGED MEN WHO LIKE TO DRESS UP. I HAVE NOTHING IN COMMON WITH THEM.

ONLY THE YOUNGEST, CALLED *OZYMANDIAS*, SEEMS INTERESTING...

IT'S NOVEMBER. THE NEWSPAPERS CALL ME A CRIMEFIGHTER, SO THE PENTAGON SAYS I MUST FIGHT CRIME. IN MOLOCH'S UNDER-GROUND VICE-DEN, THE SIGHS TURN TO SCREAMS OF TERROR.

THE MORALITY OF MY ACTIVITIES ESCAPES ME.

IT'S SEPTEMBER, 1961. JOHN KENNEDY IS SHAKING MY HAND, ASKING WHAT IT'S LIKE TO BE A SUPER-HERO. I TELL HIM HE SHOULD KNOW AND HE NODS, LAUGHING...

TWO YEARS LATER, IN DALLAS, HIS HEAD SNAPS FORWARD AND THEN BACK. TWO SHOTS...

14

IN 1969, I'M RECEIVING NEWS OF MY FATHER'S DEATH.

IN 1959, HE'S OPENING A TELEGRAM FROM THE MILITARY INFORMING HIM OF HIS SON'S ACCIDENTAL DISINTEGRATION. I NEVER CORRECT THEIR MISTAKE.

GILA FLATS CLOSES DOWN IN 1970. ON LAURIE'S TWENTIETH BIRTHDAY, WE MOVE INTO OUR NEW WASHINGTON APARTMENT.

I'VE REVEALED MY TRUE NAME TO THE PUBLIC. AFTER FATHER'S DEATH, THERE SEEMS LITTLE POINT IN CONCEALING IT.

IN JANUARY, 1971, PRESIDENT NIXON IS ASKING ME TO INTERVENE IN VIETNAM, WHILE TEN YEARS EARLIER, KENNEDY IS AVOIDING ANY MENTION OF CUBA.

LATER IN NOVEMBER, I'M TOLD THAT WALLY WEAVER HAS DIED OF CANCER, AGED 34.

IT'S MARCH. I'M IN SAIGON, BEING REINTRODUCED TO EDWARD BLAKE, THE COMEDIAN. HE WORKS MOSTLY FOR THE GOVERNMENT NOW. I SUPPOSE I DO, TOO.

BLAKE IS INTERESTING. I HAVE NEVER MET ANYONE SO DELIBERATELY AMORAL.

HE SUITS THE CLIMATE HERE: THE MADNESS, THE POINTLESS BUTCHERY...

AS I COME TO UNDERSTAND VIETNAM AND WHAT IT IMPLIES ABOUT THE HUMAN CONDITION, I ALSO REALIZE THAT FEW HUMANS WILL PERMIT THEMSELVES SUCH AN UNDERSTANDING.

BLAKE'S DIFFERENT.

HE UNDERSTANDS PERFECTLY...

...AND HE DOESN'T CARE.

19

IT'S MAY. I HAVE BEEN HERE TWO MONTHS.

THE VIETCONG ARE EXPECTED TO SURRENDER WITHIN THE WEEK. MANY HAVE GIVEN THEMSELVES UP ALREADY...

OFTEN, THEY ASK TO SURRENDER TO ME PERSONALLY, THEIR TERROR OF ME BALANCED BY AN ALMOST RELIGIOUS AWE.

I AM REMINDED OF HOW THE JAPANESE WERE REPORTED TO HAVE VIEWED THE ATOMIC BOMB, AFTER HIROSHIMA.

IT'S JUNE, V.V.N. NIGHT, AND THE COMEDIAN IS SLIDING A GUN FROM ITS HOLSTER, BLOOD STREAMING FROM HIS LACERATED FACE...

IT'S OCTOBER, 1985. DECIDING TO CREATE SOMETHING, I TURN AWAY FROM STARS THAT MAY HAVE BURNED OUT AEONS AGO. I NO LONGER WISH TO LOOK AT THEM.

I NO LONGER WISH TO LOOK AT DEAD THINGS.

20

IT'S 1975. THE PAPERS ARE FULL OF THE PRESIDENT'S PROPOSED *CONSTITUTIONAL AMENDMENT*, ALLOWING HIM TO RUN NEXT YEAR FOR A THIRD TERM.

AMIDST ALL THIS, THE UNMASKING AND RETIRE-MENT OF *OZYMANDIAS* GOES ALMOST UNNOTICED.

K?

OZYMAN QUITS 'SMART MAN IN WORLD GOES PUBLI

ADRIAN VEIDT ALIAS OZYMANDIAS

HIS REAL NAME IS *ADRIAN VEIDT*, A SELF-MADE MILLIONAIRE. AFTER RETIRING FROM ADVENTURING HE INVITES LAURIE AND ME TO VISIT HIM AT HIS ANTARCTIC RETREAT.

OOH! WHAT *IS* IT? IT'S *BEAUTIFUL!*

THAT'S *BUBASTIS*. SHE'S A GENETICALLY ALTERED *LYNX*. THEY COST RATHER A LOT TO *FEED*, I'M AFRAID.

I HADN'T REALIZED THAT *EUGENICS* WAS SO *ADVANCED* NOW...

IT'S LEAPT *FORWARD* IN THE LAST FIFTEEN YEARS. *EVERYTHING* HAS, FROM QUANTUM PHYSICS TO *TRANSPORT*.

FOR *EXAMPLE*, I UNDERSTAND THAT FAST AND SAFE *AIRSHIPS* MAY SOON BE ECONOMICALLY VIABLE...

...AND WE OWE IT ALL TO *YOU*. WITH YOUR HELP, OUR SCIENTISTS ARE LIMITED ONLY BY THEIR *IMAGINATIONS*.

AND BY THEIR *CONSCIENCES*, SURELY?

LET'S HOPE SO.

HIS EYES ARE SAD AND KNOWING. HIS SERVANTS BRING US INDONESIAN FOOD AND HE TALKS ABOUT HIS BUSINESS PLANS, ALL THE TIME FEEDING SCRAPS TO HIS BEAUTIFUL MONSTROUS CAT...

21

AUGUST 3RD, 1977: THE EMERGENCY BILL PROPOSED BY *SENATOR KEENE* HAS BEEN PASSED.

VIGILANTISM IS NOW *ILLEGAL* AGAIN, AS IT WAS BEFORE THEY ALTERED THE LAWS TO ACCOMMODATE STRATEGICALLY USEFUL TALENTS SUCH AS MYSELF.

AS LONG AS I CONTINUE TO ACT UNDER U.S. GOVERNMENT SUPERVISION, I AM EXEMPT FROM THE LAW. THEY CAN HARDLY OUTLAW ME WHEN THEIR COUNTRY'S DEFENSE RESTS IN MY HANDS.

BLAKE IS ALSO EXEMPT, SINCE HE TOO WORKS ENTIRELY FOR THE GOVERNMENT.

LATER, AFTER HIS HANDLING OF THE IRANIAN HOSTAGE SITUATION, EVEN HIS HARSHEST CRITICS FALL SILENT. LAURIE STILL HATES HIM, HOWEVER.

SHE HERSELF HAS BEEN FORCED TO RETIRE BY THE KEENE ACT, BUT HAVING NEVER REALLY ENJOYED THE LIFE, SHE DOESN'T MIND.

HER MOTHER IS MORE DISAPPOINTED THAN SHE IS.

THE NEW *NITE OWL* HAS STATED THAT HE WILL BE RETIRING, ALTHOUGH HE WILL NOT BE MAKING HIS IDENTITY PUBLIC.

LAURIE'S MET HIM SEVERAL TIMES. SHE SAYS HIS NAME IS DREIBERG.

THE ONLY OTHER ACTIVE VIGILANTE IS CALLED *RORSCHACH*, REAL NAME UNKNOWN.

HE EXPRESSES HIS FEELINGS TOWARD COMPULSORY RETIREMENT IN A NOTE LEFT OUTSIDE POLICE HEADQUARTERS ALONG WITH A DEAD MULTIPLE RAPIST.

never!

23

IT'S 1981 NOW. LAURIE AND I ARE SETTLING INTO OUR NEW QUARTERS AT THE ROCKEFELLER MILITARY RESEARCH CENTER IN NEW YORK.

IT'S WELL-EQUIPPED FOR MY WORK, BUT LAURIE FEELS WE'VE LOST OUR *PRIVACY*.

SHE'D LIKE IT HERE.

THROUGH MY BLUE FINGERS, PINK GRAINS ARE FALLING, HAPHAZARD, RANDOM, A DISORGANIZED STREAM OF SILICONE THAT SEEMS PREGNANT WITH THE POSSIBILITY OF EVERY CONCEIVABLE SHAPE...

...BUT THIS IS ILLUSION. THINGS HAVE THEIR SHAPE IN TIME, NOT SPACE ALONE. SOME MARBLE BLOCKS HAVE STATUES WITHIN THEM, EMBEDDED IN THEIR FUTURE.

IN NEW YORK, WE GO WALKING.

THE STREETS SMELL OF OZONE RATHER THAN GASOLINE. FLAT INTANGIBLE BLOTS OF GRAY SLIDE ACROSS THE SUMMER SIDEWALKS, THE SHADOWS OF OVERHEAD AIRSHIPS.

IN 1959, A CHILD IS WEEPING FOR ITS LOST BALLOONS.

ANY MOMENT NOW, JANEY'S WATCHBAND WILL BREAK. SOMEWHERE, THE FAT MAN IS ALREADY LUMBERING TOWARD THE SHOOTING GALLERY, STEPS HEAVY WITH UNWITTING DESTINY.

IT'S AUGUST, 1985. I'M WALKING THROUGH GRAND CENTRAL STATION WITH LAURIE. WE STOP AT THE NEWSSTAND AND BUY A COPY OF TIME MAGAZINE, COMMEMORATING *HIROSHIMA WEEK*.

ON THE COVER THERE IS A DAMAGED POCKET-WATCH, STOPPED AT THE INSTANT OF THE BLAST, FACE CRACKED...

...HANDS FROZEN.

24

A WORLD GROWS UP AROUND ME. AM I SHAPING IT, OR DO ITS PREDETERMINED CONTOURS GUIDE MY HAND?

IN 1945, THE BOMBS ARE FALLING ON JAPAN, THE COGS ARE FALLING ON BROOKLYN, SEEDS OF THE FUTURE, SOWN CARELESSLY....

WITHOUT ME, THINGS WOULD HAVE BEEN DIFFERENT. IF THE FAT MAN HADN'T CRUSHED THE WATCH, IF I HADN'T LEFT IT IN THE TEST CHAMBER...

AM I TO BLAME, THEN? OR THE FAT MAN? OR MY FATHER, FOR CHOOSING MY CAREER?

WHICH OF US IS RESPONSIBLE?

WHO MAKES THE WORLD?

27

DR. MANHATTAN: SUPER-POWERS AND THE SUPERPOWERS

BY PROFESSOR MILTON GLASS

Introduction

For those of us who delight in such things, the twentieth century has, in its unfolding, presented mankind with an array of behavioral paradoxes and moral conundrums hitherto unimagined and perhaps unimaginable. Science, traditional enemy of mysticism and religion, has taken on a growing understanding that the model of the universe suggested by quantum physics differs very little from the universe that Taoists and other mystics have existed in for centuries. Large numbers of young people, raised in rigidly structured and industrially oriented cultures, violently reject industrialism and seek instead some modified version of the agricultural lifestyle that their forebears (debatably) enjoyed, including extended communal families and in some instances a barter economy in miniature. Children starve while boots costing many thousands of dollars leave their mark upon the surface of the moon. We have labored long to build a heaven, only to find it populated with horrors.

It is the oldest ironies that are still the most satisfying: man, when preparing for bloody war, will orate loudly and most eloquently in the name of peace. This dichotomy is not an invention of the twentieth century, yet it is in this century that the most striking examples of the phenomena have appeared. Never before has man pursued global harmony more vocally while amassing stockpiles of weapons so devastating in their effect. The second world war—we were told—was The War To End Wars. The development of the atomic bomb is the Weapon To End Wars.

And yet wars continue. Currently, no nation on this planet is not involved in some form of armed struggle, if not against its neighbors then against internal forces. Furthermore, as ever-escalating amounts of money are poured into the pursuit of the specific weapon or conflict that will bring lasting peace, the drain on our economies creates a rundown urban landscape where crime flourishes and people are concerned less with national security than with the simple personal security needed to stop at the store late at night for a quart of milk without being mugged. The places we struggled so viciously to keep safe are becoming increasingly dangerous. The wars to end wars, the weapons to end wars, these things have failed us.

Now we have a man to end wars.

Since my association with Dr. Jonathan Osterman and the being he eventually became are well documented elsewhere, I feel I need only recap them briefly here. In 1959, in an accident that was certainly unplanned and just as certainly unrepeatable, a young American man was completely disintegrated, at least in a physical sense. Despite the absence of a body, a form of electromagnetic pattern resembling consciousness survived, and was able, in time, to rebuild an approximation of the body it had lost.

DR. MANHATTAN:

Perhaps in the process of reconstructing its corporeal form, this new and wholly original entity achieved a complete mastery of all matter; able to shape reality by the manipulation of its basic building blocks. When news of this being's phenomenal genesis was first released to the world, a certain phrase was used that has—at varying times—been attributed both to me and to others. On the newsflashes coming over our tvs on that fateful night, one sentence was repeated over and over again: 'The superman exists and he's American.'

I never said that, although I do recall saying something similar to a persistent reporter who would not leave without a quote. I presume the remark was edited or toned down so as not to offend public sensibilities; in any event, I never said 'The superman exists and he's American'. What I said was '*God* exists and he's American'. If that statement starts to chill you after a couple of moments' consideration, then don't be alarmed. A feeling of intense and crushing religious terror at the concept indicates only that you are still sane.

Since the mid-1960s, when the dazed and numbed mass consciousness first began to comprehend the significance of this new life form in humanity's midst, the political balance has changed drastically. Many people in this country feel that this is for the best. America's unquestioned military supremacy has also provided us with a certain economic leverage where we can dictate the economic policies of the western world and direct them to our advantage. There is little wonder, then, that the idea of a world run by an omnipotent God-King owing allegiance to the United States seems eminently desirable. By placing our superhuman benefactor in the position of a walking nuclear deterrent, it is assumed we have finally guaranteed lasting peace on earth. It is with this last contention that my most serious point of issue lies: I do not believe that we have a man to end wars.

I believe that we have made a man to end worlds.

The assumption that America's opponents are powerless before Dr. Manhattan, while comforting, begins to fail before closer examination. As I understand current Pentagon thinking, the conventional wisdom suggests that when faced with an insoluble problem, the Soviet Union will have no other option than acceptance of a loss of world influence culminating in its eventual defeat. It has been demonstrated, at least in well-supported theoretical terms, that Dr. Manhattan could at any time destroy large areas of Soviet territory instantly. It has been similarly theoretically demonstrated that, were a full scale nuclear assault to be launched upon America from Soviet bases in the U.S.S.R. and Europe, Dr. Manhattan would be able to deflect or disarm at least sixty percent of all incoming missiles before they had reached their targets. Against odds like that, it is argued, Russia would never risk instigating a full-scale global conflict. Since it is not in America's interests to promote such a conflict, does that mean that global peace is once and finally assured? No. It does not.

For one thing, it is an assumption based upon the belief that American psychology and its Soviet counterpart are interchangeable. To understand the Russian attitude to the possibility of a third world war one must first understand their attitude to the second. In WWII, none of the allied powers fought so bitterly or sustained such losses as did the Russians. It was Hitler's lack of success in his assault upon the

III

Soviet heartland that assured his eventual defeat, and though it was paid for mostly by Soviet lives, the entire world reaped the benefits. In time, the Russian contribution to the war effort has been downplayed and dismissed—most noticeably as our political differences became wider—as we glorified our own contribution while forgetting that of our estranged former allies. The Russians, however, have not forgotten. There are still those who remember the horror of a war fought on their soil, and almost certainly there are members of the Politburo in that category. From my reading of various pronouncements made by the Russian high command over the years, I am convinced that they will never again permit their nation to be threatened in a similar manner, *no matter what the cost.*

The presence of a deterrent such as Dr. Manhattan has doubtless curbed Soviet adventurism, as there have been numerous occasions when the U.S.S.R. has had to step down over some issue rather than risk escalation into a war it certainly could not win. Often, these reversals have been humiliating, and this has perhaps fostered the illusion that the Soviets will suffer such indignities endlessly. This is a misconception, for there is indeed another option available.

That option is Mutually Assured Destruction. Stated simply, Dr. Manhattan cannot stop all the Soviet warheads from reaching American soil, even a greatly reduced percentage would still be more than enough to effectively end the organic life in the northern hemisphere. The suggestion that the presence of a superhuman has inclined the world more towards peace is refudiated by the sharp increase in both Russian and American nuclear stockpiles since the advent of Dr. Manhattan. Infinite destruction divided by two or ten or twenty is still infinite destruction. If threatened with eventual domination, would the Soviets pursue this unquestionably suicidal course? Yes. Given their history and their view of the world, I believe that they would.

Our current administration believes otherwise. They continually push their unearned advantage until American influence comes uncomfortably close to key areas of Soviet interest. It is as if—with a real live Deity on their side—our leaders have become intoxicated with a heady draught of Omnipotence-by-Association, without realizing just how his very existence has deformed the lives of every living creature on the face of this planet.

This is true in a domestic sense as well as a broader, international one. The technology that Dr. Manhattan has made possible has changed the way we think about our clothes, our food, our travel. We drive in electric cars and travel in leisure and comfort in clean, economical airships. Our entire culture has had to contort itself to accommodate the presence of something more than human, and we have all felt the results of this. The evidence surrounds us, in our everyday lives and on the front pages of the newspapers we read. One single being has been allowed to change the entire world, pushing it closer to its eventual destruction in the process. The Gods now walk amongst us, affecting the lives of every man, woman and child on the planet in a direct way rather than through mythology and the reassurances of faith. The safety of a whole world rests in the hands of a being far beyond what we understand to be human.

We are all of us living in the shadow of Manhattan.

DR. MANHATTAN:

HWUH ...?

H-HELLO?

WHO'S THERE?

1

C'MON... I HEARD A *NOISE*. I KNOW *SOMEBODY'S* THERE...

HELLO?

UH-HUH.

I SEE.

WELL, OKAY...

OKAY, IF THAT'S HOW IT *IS*...

IF THAT'S HOW YOU WANT TO PLAY IT.

YOU THINK I'M *SCARED*, HUH?

YOU THINK I'M *SCARED* OF SOME SHAKY LITTLE JUNKIE WITH A SWITCHBLADE?

HUH?

IS THAT WHAT YOU THINK, THAT I'M *SCARED*?

HELLO?

2

BeHind
You.
:Jr.

3

FEARFUL SYMMETRY

I ...I WASN'T...

I WASN'T GOING TO POINT IT AT YOU.

HHUHHH!

NO, PLEASE, WHAT ...?

GUN.

NO LICENSE.

I CHECKED.

VERY BAD.

4

Panel 1: WE NEED TO KNOW *EVERYTHING*, MRS. HIRSCH....

Panel 2: WAR. HE SAID THERE WAS GONNA BE WAR WITH THE *RUSSIANS*. SAID HE WANTED TO *SPARE* THE LITTLE ONES.

Panel 3: DOMINIQUE, SHE KEPT SAYING "*WAH*", WHICH IS, LIKE, "*WAR*". SHE'S JUST *THREE*, SHE *REPEATS* THINGS. AND THEN ... OH.

OOOHHHHHH.

OKAY, MRS. HIRSCH. NO MORE *QUESTIONS*. OFFICER CAPALDI WILL DRIVE YOU TO THE *HOSPITAL*.

Panel 4: JESUS. WHAT *HAPPENED*?

GUY WORRIED ABOUT *NUCLEAR WAR*. KILLED BOTH KIDS IN FRONT OF THEIR MOM, THEN OPENED HIS *JUGULAR*.

THERE'S GONNA BE *MORE* LIKE THIS.

Panel 5: YEAH. WELL, ME, I THINK IT'S *ASTROLOGICAL*. *HALLEY'S COMET* IS COMING BACK AROUND NOW. THAT'S AN OMEN OF DOOM.

YEAH. SO'S *RUSSIA* INVADING *AFGHANISTAN*.

Panel 6: AHH, THAT'LL BLOW OVER. WORLD WAR THREE, IT'LL NEVER HAPPEN. NOBODY'S *CRAZY* ENOUGH.

BOY. WHAT DID HE USE ON *THESE*?

KITCHEN KNIFE. THEIR NAMES WERE CLARE AND DOMINIQUE.

Panel 7: NICE *NAMES*. SORTA *FILM STAR* NAMES.

YEAH.

SO, YA WANNA GO GET SOME *BREAKFAST*?

YEAH.

Panel 8: GOOD. LISTEN, DON'T LET THIS RUIN YOUR DAY. THESE *PSYCH-OUTS* ARE MOSTLY *MEDIA INSPIRED*.

THE MEDIA INSPIRES *BOREDOM* NOT WAKING UP ONE MONDAY MORNING AND BUTCHERING YOUR *KIDS*.

THAT TAKES SOMETHING *ELSE*, MAN.

Panel 9: THAT TAKES A WHOLE DIFFERENT *KIND* OF INSPIRATION.

7

RORSCHACH'S JOURNAL. OCTOBER 21ST, 1985 =

Woken at eleven by shouting outside. Disturbed to find I had fallen asleep without removing the skin from my head. Tireder than I thought. Should be more careful.

Across street, boys with spray cans were defacing abandoned building. Memorized their descriptions, then prepared for work.

First, peeled off face, folded it, hid inside jacket. Without my face, nobody knows.

Nobody knows who I am.

On way out of room, met landlady. Usual complaints re hygiene and rent. There were purple bite marks on her fat white neck. Fresh ones.

She reminds me of my mother.

Out in street, inspected defaced building: silhouette picture in doorway, man and woman, possibly indulging in sexual foreplay.

Didn't like it. Makes doorway look haunted.

On fortieth and seventh, saw Dreiberg and Juspeczyk leaving diner. They didn't know me.

An affair, perhaps? Did Juspeczyk engineer Dr. Manhattan's exile to make room for Dreiberg? Also, she hated Comedian. Must investigate further.

Entering diner, bought coffee then sat watching my maildrop, immediately across street.

Passers-by made various deposits: candy wrappers, newspapers, a pair of Keds strangled by own laces, tongues lolling out horribly.

This city is an animal, fierce and complicated. To understand it I read its droppings, its scents, the movement of its parasites...

I sat watching the trashcan, and New York opened its heart to me.

11

15

16

DURING THE AFTERNOON, I DOZED FITFULLY, MY ENEMIES' HIDEOUS BANNER FLAPPING DISMALLY IN MY DREAMS.

WAR, CHILD MURDER, ATTEMPTED ASSASSINATION... THIS FRONT PAGE IS A NIGHTMARE!

SOMEBODY CHOPS UP THEIR KIDS, SOMEBODY ELSE SHOOTS AT ADRIAN VEIDT...

I MEAN, WHO'D WANNA KILL A GUY LIKE THAT?

THAT DEATHS-HEAD BANNER, IT FLIES ABOVE US ALL...

...AND THE HEADS NAILED TO THE SHIP'S BLACK PROW, THOSE HEADS ARE OUR HEADS.

IT'S LIKE, IF SOMEBODY WANTS TO OFF A SAINT LIKE VEIDT, WHAT CHANCE DO ANY OF US GOT?

VEIDT'S A REAL HERO. DID CHARITY WORK. REVEALED HIS NAME LIKE HE HAD NOTHING TO HIDE.

TRULY, WHOEVER WE ARE, WHEREVER WE RESIDE, WE EXIST UPON THE WHIM OF MURDERERS.

JEEZ. WHERE'S IT GUNNA END?

I AWOKE AT DUSK AND DRANK A LITTLE SALT WATER. I HAVE HEARD THAT ON LESS THAN A PINT DAILY, A MAN MIGHT SURVIVE.

HELL, NO WONDER PEOPLE GO CRAZY.

LIKE THIS GUY KILLED HIS KIDS. A WEEK AGO, THAT WAS A NORMAL FAMILY.

YOU NEVER KNOW. YOU NEVER KNOW WHAT'S BEARING DOWN ON YOU.

INSTITUTE FOR EXTRASPATIAL STUDIES

BENEATH MY RAFT, SOMETHING MOVED.

IRRATIONALLY, MY FIRST THOUGHT WAS OF THE CORPSES, BURSTING THEIR BONDS, ATTEMPTING TO CLAMBER UP INTO THE AIR AND DRYNESS, BUT NO. SOMETHING HAD BRUSHED BENEATH ME.

I BET THERE'S ALL KINDA STUFF WE NEVER NOTICE...

I MEAN, ALL WE SEE IS WHAT'S ON THE SURFACE.

MY PLATFORM LURCHED AGAIN. AHEAD, IN THE DARKENING WATER, I HEARD A SPLASH. SHADOWY FORMS APPROACHED. WERE THEY BOATS COME TO RESCUE ME?

...UNTIL IT'S TOO LATE.

NO, NOT BOATS.

FINS.

17

GOOD READERS, KNOW THIS: HADES IS WET. HADES IS LONELY.

TEETH THAT SEEMED TO MOVE INDEPENDENTLY OF THE LIPS TORE AT MY RAFT'S SUPPORTS. TINY PREHISTORIC EYES GLISTENED, SEEMING MAD WITH RAGE EVEN IN REPOSE.

WHATEVER WAS BENEATH MY BOAT COMMENCED A VIOLENT THRASHING, ALMOST SPILLING ME AMONGST THE GNAWING HORRORS.

I CLUNG TO MY MAST AS THE PLATFORM TILTED FURTHER. THE WATER BEGAN TO BOIL WHITE. SOMETHING WAS SURFACING.

HOW SHALL I DESCRIBE IT? IT WAS MASSIVE, LIKE NO SHARK I'D EVER HEARD TELL OF, WITH SKIN NEITHER BLACK NOR WHOLLY WHITE, BUT A PALE AND MOTTLED YELLOW.

FURTHER, IT WAS ENTANGLED IN MY ROPES.

TERRIFIED LEST IT SHOULD RE-SUBMERGE AND DRAG ME WITH IT, I FELL TO MY KNEES CLUTCHING A SPLINTER OF MAST THAT HAD SNAPPED OFF IN MY HAND.

THE SHARK'S STAINED MARBLE EYE LOOKED UP AT ME...

...AND, IN THAT INSTANT, WE KNEW EACH OTHER.

HALF BLIND; HALF DEAD; WHOLLY DERANGED BY AGONY; THE YELLOW LEVIATHAN ATTEMPTED TO SWIM AWAY, DRAGGING MY RAFT IN ITS BLOODY WAKE.

I HUNG ON DESPERATELY, CURSING IN THE BITTER, STINGING SPRAY.

20

The following is reprinted from chapter five of the Treasure Island Treasury Of Comics (Flint Editions, New York, 1984) with permission of the author and publishers.

As discussed in our last chapter, the close of the 1950s saw E.C.'s line of Pirate titles dominating the marketplace from a near unassailable position. The brief surge of anti-comic book sentiment in the mid-fifties, while it could conceivably have damaged E.C. as a company, had instead come to nothing and left them stronger as a result. With the government of the day coming down squarely on the side of comic books in an effort to protect the image of certain comic book-inspired agents in their employ, it was as if the comic industry had suddenly been given the blessing of Uncle Sam himself—or at least J. Edgar Hoover. Unsurprisingly, as one of the few companies to anticipate the coming massive boom in pirate-related material, E.C. flourished and their hold upon the field remained unchallenged.

Until May, 1960. That date saw the first publication of an extraordinary new title from National Comics, now DC. The book was called 'Tales of the Black Freighter', and while its sales never

A MAN ON FIFTEEN DEAD MEN'S CHESTS

quite topped those of the E.C. giants such as PIRACY and BUCCANEERS, in terms of critical acclaim and influence upon later books of the same type, TALES OF THE BLACK FREIGHTER made an impression upon the comic book landscape that remains to this day. Indeed, with DC comics currently reprinting the first classic thirty issues of the title and apparently meeting with considerable success, it would seem that its impact remains undiluted despite the quarter century that has elapsed since the original publication.

What exactly was it that made TALES OF THE BLACK FREIGHTER so special? Despite the fact that nowadays most people are attracted by the controversy surrounding the later issues of the book, it should be remembered that this title was very popular from the outset. So: What was it that fascinated all those thousands of readers in the first place?

Well, to begin with, it was almost certainly the artwork of Joe Orlando, who drew the entire book from its first issue through issue nine, with the exception of GALAPAGOS JONES, a rather insipid back-up feature that lasted until issue six. Orlando, having been successfully tempted away from his well-received run of 'SARGASSO SEA STORIES' in E.C.'s PIRACY by National editor Julius Schwartz, was regarded as a star amongst pirate artists, and a prize catch. Having adapted more smoothly from

science fiction and horror to the different atmospheric demands of pirate stories than many of his E.C. contemporaries, he was perhaps the best respected artist in a rapidly burgeoning field, and fans awaited the first issue of TALES OF THE BLACK FREIGHTER with relish.

Nor were they disappointed. The first issue is classic Orlando. The script—by then-newcomer Max Shea—while sturdy enough, is cliched and predictable in comparison with the work that Shea did later, and in that first issue was easily outshone by the darkly compelling majesty of Orlando's textures, shadows and faces.

The story served as an introduction to the vessel that lent the book its title, and which was itself apparently borrowed from a ship referred to in Brecht and Weill's 'THREEPENNY OPERA'. In that first story, three men with different paths through life have all been led to the same dockside tavern in search of work. The place is deserted save for a shadowy innkeeper who serves them ale in silence and the large, dark figure of a sea captain who sits at the next table and listens to them recount their stories to each other.

The stories are recounted as small, self-contained tales within the larger narrative that frames them, and are all effective if predictable twist-ending yarns that reveal the various tellers to be utterly unprincipled and worthless creatures capable of almost any act of treachery. Overhearing their stories, the sea captain says he is impressed and offers them passage upon his ship. By the time the men are aboard the ship and have noticed the dreadful, deathly smell that seems to exude from the ship's timbers, it is too late. The three hapless sailors learn that the ship is a vessel from Hell itself to take on board the souls of evil men so that they may walk its blood-stained decks for all eternity.

The identity of the captain is never made clear—is he meant to be Satan, or is he himself a victim of the ship? But this scarcely matters when confronted with Orlando's breathtaking rendition. From the marvelous scene in the first man's story where two ghouls fight to the death with shovels in the worm-infested tunnels beneath a churchyard, right through the haunting and evocative final shots of the horrible black ship drifting away into the white mist, the art is breathtaking, conveying a tangible sense of doom and evil even in those places where the writing fails to do so.

With the issues that followed, Orlando's art continued to shine while the scripts supplied by Shea

JOE ORLANDO, CIRCA 1953

also began to gradually improve in quality as the writer became used to the medium. With rapidly increasing confidence, Shea began attempting ideas for stories which at the time seemed wildly radical and innovative. The third issue's story, "Between Breaths", is told from the viewpoint of a man who is drowning, alternating between memories of his past life as they flash before his bulging eyes and horrific descriptions of what it is like to drown. Even read today, the story induces an almost tangible sense of suffocation, so that finishing the story and putting the book down is actually a relief. The closing images, with a multitude of dead and drowned men walking across the ocean bed towards the anchor rope of the Black Freighter which they climb to take their rightful positions on board the ship, remain some of Orlando's most haunting work on the series.

By issue five, reader reaction was obviously in favor of the title, and the praise seemed to be divided equally between Orlando and Shea. According to insiders, receiving fan mail for the first time in his life had an adverse effect upon the writer, who began to see himself as the driving force of the book, becoming increasingly resentful of Orlando's clearly important role and harassing the artist with impossibly detailed panel descriptions and endless carping requests for revisions of artwork already drawn.

Despite growing friction within the creative team, both lasted on TALES OF THE BLACK FREIGHTER until the ninth issue, when Orlando asked Schwartz to take him off the book, citing the ego of the writer as being the major factor in his decision. During those nine issues they crafted many memorable stories together, including the most famous of all, "The Shanty of Edward Teach", in issue seven. In this story, narrated in rhyme by the dead pirate Edward Teach (otherwise known as Blackbeard), we first begin to see the dark and pessimistic moral sensibilities showing that were later to form most of Shea's work on the series. These are more than adequately matched by Orlando's artwork, and there can be few readers of that period who will forget the heart-stopping close-up shot of Blackbeard, portrayed as violent and leering evil incarnate, in which he seems to look out at the reader and remind them that their own position is perhaps no more noble than Teach's own: "I tread a lurching timber world, a reeking salt-caked hell; and yet, perhaps, no worse a world than yours, where bishops stroll through charnel yards with pomanders to smell; where vile men thrive and love crawls on all fours."

After Orlando's departure, the art for the series was taken over by a relatively unknown but supremely capable artist named Walt Feinberg, previously best known for his work upon numerous western titles where he would often provide excellent fill-in issues that nevertheless seemed

THIS CABIN-LAD'S GROWN HAGGARD, SO IN THE POT HE GOES AND FROM HIS SKIN WE'LL MAKE A LITTLE DRUM TO BEAT AS WE FIRE HUMAN HEADS FROM CANNONS AT OUR FOES. AND SET THE SEAS ABLAZE WITH BURNING RUM.

I TREAD A LURCHING TIMBER WORLD; A REEKING, SALT-CAKED HELL; AND YET, PERHAPS, NO WORSE A WORLD THAN YOURS, WHERE BISHOPS STROLL THROUGH CHARNEL YARDS WITH POMANDERS TO SMELL; WHERE VILE MEN THRIVE AND LOVE CRAWLS ON ALL FOURS.

to go unnoticed when slotted in between the work of great western comic artists such as Gil Kane and Alex Toth. Despite having Orlando's early work on the series to live up to, on TALES OF THE BLACK FREIGHTER, Feinberg was finally given a chance to shine. For some reason, there are few incidents on record relating friction between Feinberg and Shea, and indeed the two of them continued to work together on the book until issue thirty-one, at which point Shea quit (perhaps the moody and temperamental writer was making a deliberate effort to control his behavior, having been taught an expensive lesson by Orlando's departure).

In any event the next twenty or so issues of the book became every bit as much instant classics as the Orlando issues had, a fact not hindered by Shea's gradually developing skill as a writer.

The stories that came from his pen in this period are uniformly dark and sinister, balancing metaphysical terrors against an unnerving sense of reality, particularly when applied to matters of mortality or sexuality. Readers who came to the series expecting a good rousing tale of swashbuckling were either repulsed or fascinated by what were often perverse and blackly lingering comments upon the human condition. Tales such as "The Figurehead", which deal unflinchingly with male homosexuality, and the harrowing "Marooned" spring most readily to mind.

In "Marooned", a two-part story occupying issues twenty-three and twenty-four of the book's run, we see Feinberg and Shea at their blood-freezing best. Unusual in that it is a one-character story narrated mostly in captions, "Marooned" tells the story of a young mariner whose vessel is wrecked by the Black Freighter before it can return to its hometown and warn it of the hell-ship's approach. Cast adrift on an uninhabited island with only his dead shipmates for company, we experience the frantic mariner's torment at the knowledge that while he is trapped on his island, the bestial crew of the Freighter are surely bearing down upon his town, his home, his wife and his children. Driven by his burning desire to avert this calamity, we see the mariner finally

escape from the island by what may be one of the most striking and horrific devices thus far in pirate comic books: digging up the recently buried and gas-bloated corpses of his shipmates, the mariner lashes them together and uses them as the floats on an improvised raft on which he hopes to reach the mainland (hence the title of this chapter.) On reaching the mainland safely

upon his horrific craft we see the increasingly distraught and dishevelled mariner trying desperately to reach his home, even resorting to murder to acquire a horse for himself. In the final scenes, thanks to the skillful interplay of text and pictures, we see that the mariner, though he has escaped from his island, is in the end marooned from the rest of humanity in a much more terrible fashion.

Problems set in for the book around issue twenty-five, when Shea began his controversial

TALES OF THE
BLACK
FREIGHTER

run of issues based around the contents of plundered books in the library of the Freighter's captain, including banned tomes supposedly originally headed for eternal suppression within the vaults of Vatican city when stolen en route by the pirates. Described as 'blatantly pornographic', four of the projected five stories were rejected by DC, which brought about the argument in which Shea quit the book and comics as well, going on to write such classic novels as the twice-filmed FOGDANCING.

At the time of this writing, Shea's whereabouts are unknown. In circumstances as strange as those in any of his stories, the writer apparently vanished from his home one morning and has not been seen since, although police are continuing their inquiries. In his wake he leaves not only a string of excellent novels and screenplays, but also an exemplary run of pirate stories which today fetch mint prices of almost a thousand dollars according to the Overstreet Guide. Stories there to be rediscovered and reexamined, like so many of the fascinating sunken treasures lurking just beneath the surface of this fabulous and compelling genre.

CHAPTER VI

THE ABYSS GAZES ALSO

3

ONCE HIS *HOME LIFE* HAD BEEN INVESTIGATED, HE WAS REMOVED FROM HIS MOTHER'S CUSTODY AND PUT INTO *CARE.* AWAY FROM HER, HE SEEMED TO *IMPROVE.*

EXCELLING AT SCHOOLWORK, KOVACS GREW INTO A *BRIGHT* BUT UNUSUALLY *QUIET* CHILD.

MAL?

EVEN IN 1956, WHEN INFORMED OF HIS MOTHER'S BRUTAL MURDER, HE RESTRICTED HIS COMMENTS TO *ONE WORD:*

"*GOOD.*"

MAL, IT'S *LATE.* ARE YOU *DONE* WITH THIS *RORSCHACH* CASE YET?

NOT *RORSCHACH.* WALTER *KOVACS.* RORSCHACH'S AN UNHEALTHY *FANTASY* PERSONALITY. Y'KNOW, HE WOULDN'T *ANSWER* TO ANYTHING ELSE DURING HIS *BAIL* HEARING?

ON THE *NEWS* HE SOUNDED *FRIGHTENING.* DON'T GET TOO *WRAPPED UP* IN THIS ONE, MAL. IT MIGHT RUIN YOUR *CHEERFUL* DISPOSITION.

GLORIA, I'M TOO *FAT* AND CONTENTED FOR ANYTHING TO RUIN MY DISPOSITION...

...ALTHOUGH SOME OF THE STUFF ABOUT HIS *EARLY LIFE,* FANTASIES ABOUT A FATHER HE NEVER *KNEW*...

SHH. LEAVE IT AT THE *OFFICE.* YOU GOT A NICE LIFE, *I* GOT A NICE LIFE. NOBODY ELSE MATTERS.

I GUESS NOT. IT'S JUST THAT HE'S *WITHDRAWN* AND *DEPRESSED,* AND I REALLY FEEL I CAN *GUIDE* HIM *OUT* OF IT.

WELL, IF ANYBODY CAN, IT'S *YOU*...

YOU'RE THE *NICEST,* MOST *POSITIVE* PERSON I *KNOW. THAT'S* WHY YOU GOTTA LOOK *AFTER* YOURSELF. I MEAN, ARE YOU *SURE* YOU'RE *SAFE* WITH THIS *KOVACS* GUY?

DON'T WORRY. WHILE HE'S AT *SING-SING* AWAITING *TRIAL* HE'S UNDER *HEAVY GUARD.* HE'S NO *THREAT.*

NOT ANY *MORE.*

WELL, LET'S HOPE NOT. NOW C'MON.... FORGET WORK. IT'S A BEAUTIFUL *NIGHT...*

"LET'S SEE IF WE CAN MAKE IT LAST *FOREVER.*"

8

THE GUARDS INTERVENED, DRAGGING KOVACS AWAY TO SOLITARY AND THE OTHER MAN TO THE PRISON HOSPITAL.

ACCORDING TO THE DEPUTY WARDEN, HIS BURNS WERE HORRIFIC. HOT COOKING FAT... I DON'T LIKE TO THINK ABOUT IT.

AS THEY DRAGGED HIM AWAY, RORSCHACH SPOKE TO THE OTHER INMATES.

HE SAID "NONE OF YOU UNDER-STAND. *I'M* NOT LOCKED UP IN HERE WITH *YOU*. *YOU'RE* LOCKED UP IN HERE WITH *ME*."

MY EARLIER OPTIMISM WAS OBVIOUSLY UNFOUNDED. HE'S GETTING WORSE.

SO AM I. JUST READ BACK WHAT I'VE WRITTEN ABOVE. THE SIXTH LINE DOWN SHOULD READ "KOVACS SPOKE TO THE OTHER INMATES."

KOVACS.

NOT RORSCHACH.

MAL? YOU'RE *NEVER* GONNA SLEEP WITH ALL THAT *COFFEE* INSIDE YOU.

OH. HI, GLORIA. ACTUALLY, I WASN'T PLANNING ON SLEEPING JUST YET.

THIS KOVACS CASE. YOU KNOW ...REQUIRES A LOT OF *ATTENTION*...

REMEMBER LAST *NIGHT*, MAL? WHEN *I* REQUIRED ATTENTION?

GLORIA, *PLEASE!* THEN WAS *THEN*, NOW IS *NOW*...

...AND FRANKLY I THINK IT'S UNFAIR OF YOU TO BRING UP *SEX* WHEN YOU KNOW I NEED TO *WORK*.

OH. WELL, MAYBE I JUST SOMETIMES NOTICE HOW OFTEN YOU BRING UP *WORK* WHEN YOU KNOW I NEED *SEX*.

GOOD NIGHT, MAL.

WAIT! GLORIA, WHAT DO YOU *MEAN*? COME *BACK* HERE. WE CAN *TALK*...

"YOU'RE LOCKED UP IN HERE WITH ME," HE SAID.

HE'S RIGHT.

ABSOLUTELY RIGHT.

13

FROM THE NOTES OF DR. MALCOLM LONG. OCTOBER 27TH, 1985 =

HIS LAST WORDS TODAY WERE "WE DO IT BECAUSE WE ARE COMPELLED."

BUT HE NEVER SAYS WHAT IT *IS* THAT COMPELS HIM. IT'S NOT HIS *CHILDHOOD*, HIS *MOTHER* OR *KITTY GENOVESE*. THOSE THINGS JUST MADE HIM *OVER-REACT* TO THE *INJUSTICE* IN THE WORLD.

THEY'RE NOT WHAT SENT HIM OVER ITS EDGE.

THEY'RE NOT WHAT TURNED HIM INTO RORSCHACH.

IT'S AS IF CONTINUAL CONTACT WITH SOCIETY'S *GRIM* ELEMENTS HAS SHAPED HIM INTO SOMETHING *GRIMMER*, SOMETHING EVEN *WORSE*.

IF ONLY I COULD CONVINCE HIM THAT LIFE ISN'T *LIKE* THAT. THE *WORLD* ISN'T LIKE THAT.

I'M *POSITIVE* IT ISN'T.

BOUGHT A GAZETTE ON WAY HOME, INCLUDING A SMALL PIECE ABOUT KOVACS WHICH THE NEWSVENDOR POINTED OUT EXCITEDLY. I GUESS HE DOES THAT TO EVERYBODY.

APPARENTLY, KOVACS VISITED HIS NEWSSTAND REGULARLY.

THE COINCIDENCE IS TRIVIAL, BUT UNSETTLING.

SO WAS THE FRONT PAGE. RUSSIAN TANKS HAVE ENTERED PAKISTAN.

ON SEVENTH AVENUE, SOMEONE HAD SPRAYED SILHOUETTE FIGURES ONTO THE WALL. IT REMINDED ME OF THE PEOPLE DISINTEGRATED AT *HIROSHIMA*, LEAVING ONLY THEIR INDELIBLE SHADOWS.

AT HOME, GLORIA SEEMED ANXIOUS TO SWEETEN THINGS AFTER YESTERDAY AND TOLD ME SHE'D INVITED RANDY AND DIANA TO DINNER TOMORROW.

WAS TOO EXHAUSTED TO TAKE IN ALL THE DETAILS AND SUGGESTED AN EARLY NIGHT.

16

20

SHOCK OF IMPACT RAN ALONG MY ARM. JET OF WARMTH SPATTERED ON CHEST, LIKE HOT FAUCET.

IT WAS KOVACS WHO SAID "MOTHER" THEN, MUFFLED UNDER LATEX. IT WAS KOVACS WHO CLOSED HIS EYES.

IT WAS RORSCHACH WHO OPENED THEM AGAIN.

ACCORDING TO MY INFORMANT, MAN USING PREMISES NAMED GERALD GRICE.

OUT DRINKING WHEN I CALLED. RETURNED TO DRESSMAKERS AT TEN FORTY-FIVE.

DARK BY THEN.

DARK AS IT GETS.

21

22

DIANA REMEMBERED THAT THEIR BABYSITTER HAD TO BE HOME EARLY AND THEY LEFT SOON AFTER DINNER.

GLORIA WENT INTO THE BEDROOM. I FOLLOWED HER. SHE WALKED OUT AGAIN, INTO THE HALL.

I SAT ON THE BED.

SHE CAME IN, WEARING HER COAT, SUBJECTED ME TO A LOT OF CRUDE SEXUAL INSULTS, WENT OUT. THE FRONT DOOR SLAMMED.

WHY DO WE ARGUE? LIFE'S SO FRAGILE, A SUCCESSFUL VIRUS CLINGING TO A SPECK OF MUD, SUSPENDED IN ENDLESS NOTHING.

NEXT WEEK, I COULD BE PUTTING HER INTO A GARBAGE SACK, PLACING HER OUTSIDE FOR COLLECTION.

I SAT ON THE BED.

I LOOKED AT THE RORSCHACH BLOT.

I TRIED TO PRETEND IT LOOKED LIKE A SPREADING TREE, SHADOWS POOLED BENEATH IT, BUT IT DIDN'T.

IT LOOKED MORE LIKE A DEAD CAT I ONCE FOUND, THE FAT, GLISTENING GRUBS WRITHING BLINDLY, SQUIRMING OVER EACH OTHER, FRANTICALLY TUNNELING AWAY FROM THE LIGHT.

BUT EVEN THAT IS AVOIDING THE REAL HORROR.

THE HORROR IS THIS: IN THE END, IT IS SIMPLY A PICTURE OF EMPTY MEANINGLESS BLACKNESS.

WE ARE ALONE.

THERE IS NOTHING ELSE.

Battle not with monsters, lest ye become a monster,

and if you gaze into the abyss, the abyss gazes also into you.

—Friedrich Wilhelm Nietzsche

Form 2-18

WALTER J. KOVACS

New York
Police Department

MANHATTAN

FOR INTER-DEPARTMENTAL USE ONLY

(Please type or print clearly)

Name KOVACS, Walter Joseph

Address TRANSIENT

Born 3/21/40

Mothers name KOVACS, Sylvia Joanna (née GLICK)

Fathers name Unknown

LEFT THUMB PRINT	RIGHT THUMB PRINT

DETAILS OF ARREST   COPIES:

Walter Joseph Kovacs, A.K.A. RORSCHACH, was arrested on the night of Monday, October 21st when a squadron of police officers led by Detectives FINE and BOURQUIN surrounded the house of EDGAR WILLIAM JACOBI, A.K.A. EDGAR WILLIAM VAUGHN, A.K.A. WILLIAM EDGAR BRIGHT, A.K.A. MOLOCH, following an anonymous tip: Kovacs, who was on the premises at the time, injured two police officers while resisting arrest. Officer SHAW was admitted to the hospital with minor burns, while Officer Greaves, who was shot at point blank range with a gas-powered grappling gun, has a shattered sternum and is still on the hospital's critical list as of this writing (10/22/85).

When the house was explored, the body of Edgar Jacobi was discovered in the kitchen, shot through the head. The murder weapon was found less than two feet away, and although there were no fingerprints on the gun it should be remembered that since Kovacs was wearing gloves when arrested, this lack of prints is hardly remarkable. Although Kovacs has denied the murder of Jacobi, given his previous history of violence against other criminals and his location in the murder house at the time, few other conclusions seem possible. Curiously, Kovacs has not denied the two other murders attributed to him, those of GERALD ANTHONY GRICE, unemployed, in the summer of 1975, and of wanted multiple rapist HARVEY CHARLES FURNISS two years later in the summer of 1977, immediately following the passage of the Keene Act into law.

At the time of his arrest, the contents of Kovacs' pockets were as follows: 1 battery powered flashlight; 5 individually wrapped cubes 'Sweet Chariot' chewing sugar; 1 map New York underground and subway system, dated 1968 with recent alterations drawn in with a red ballpoint pen; withered remains one red rose; one dollar fifty-nine cents in assorted loose change; one pencil; one notebook, pages filled with what is either an elaborate cypher or handwriting too cramped and eccentric to be legible; one broken bottle 'Nostalgia' cologne for men, possibly broken during leap from Jacobi's second story window during arrest; a residue of ground black pepper.

(If second sheet is needed refer to Form 6-2)

EARLY HISTORY: A SUMMARY:

Sylvia Kovacs came to New York from Ohio in the spring of 1935 with her husband, Peter Joseph Kovacs, whom she divorced in 1937 amidst mutual accusations of adultery and mental cruelty. After the divorce she had no further contact with her former husband, and for the next three years, she lived in a number of low-rent apartments, both alone and with a number of male acquaintances. Exactly when she drifted into prostitution as a means of meeting her mounting debts is uncertain, but it seems likely that her last semi-permanent relationship was with the true father of Walter Kovacs, who left her two months before the baby was born. Mrs. Kovacs was either unable or unwilling to provide any details concerning him other than that his name was 'Charlie'. Sicne shortly after the birth of her son we see Mrs. Kovacs' first arrest on charges of prostitution, we can perhaps assume that the addi- tional cost of keeping an infant child may have been what necessitated this new occupation, and perhaps also speculate as to whether the above factors were the cause of the resentment and cruelty which Sylvia Kovacs showed to her son as he grew older.

In the July of 1951, the boy was admitted into care after vi- ciously attacking two older boys in the street, partially blinding one of them. When questioned, Kovacs refused to talk about what had caused him to attack the boys, so it must be presumed that it was an unprovoked assault. Nerertheless, investigation of the circumstances the boy lived in revealed that he was regularly beaten and exposed to the worst excesses of a prostitutes lifestyle, and it was decide to place the child under care. He was admitted to the Lillian Charlton Home for Problem Children in New Jersey, where he remained until 1956, when it was decided that he was intelligent and stable enough to func- tion in normal society. During his time at hte home, removed from his mother's negative influence, Kovacs did very well at schoolwork, excelling particularly in the fields of literature and religious ed- uscation as well as possessing an impressive skill in the areas of gymnastics and amateur boxing. While quiet and shy, especially with women, Kovacs was capable of long and well-reasoned conversations with hi classmates and instructors, and struck most peop as a serious but likeable child who was merely a bit withdrawn.

this aside, it is clear that his loathin of his mother remained undiminished. Shortly before Kovacs left the Charlton home in 1956, news was received that his mother, who had never made any attempt to contact her child and who ha continued to become further involved in the worl of small-time vice, had been murdered. Her body had been found in a back alleyway in the South Bronx, the cause of death being the forced ing estion of Drano cleaning fluid.A man named George Paterson, Mrs. Kovacs' pimp, was later charged

New York State Psychiatric Hospital
West Branch

with her murder. When the news was broken to Walter Kovacs, then aged six-
teen, his only comment was 'Good.' Shortly after this , Kovacs left
the home to take up residence in the first of a series of small apartments
and also take up full employment in a menial capacity within the garment
industry, an occupation he apparently remained in up until the mid-
seventies, maintaining a dual life between his daytime employment and
his nocturnal activities in the guise of 'Rorschach'.
    Very little physical evidence existsthat gives a clear insight
into the psychology of this troubled man. Some police officers have
tentatively identified hima s a prophet-of-doom sandwich-board man
seen locally over the last several years, but as Kovacs refuses to divulge his current address, if any, this is not provable at such an early stage in the investigation. Similarly, material relating to his early
years is scarce, although I have been able to obtain photocopies of
two pieces written by Kovacs during his stay at the Charlton Home, one
being an essay written on the set topic of 'My Parents' when Kovacs
was eleven, the other being a transcription of Kovacs' verbal recounting
of a nightmare he suffered when he was thirteen.

Charlton Home

                                                    by Walter Kovacs

My Parents

    I have two parents, although actually, I don't have any. I never see my mom,
but that's okay, although I would like to see my dad sometimes. I have never met
my dad and I would sure like to. He had to leave our house when I wasn't even
born, I guess because he couldn't get along with my mother. I would of done the
same if I was him.

    I used to ask my mom about my dad, but she doesn't talk much about him. His
name was charlie, which is short for Charles although it has the same number of
letters. She says she doesn't know his second name although how can you live with
somebodt if you don't know who they are? It is just stupid.

    My mom told me she threw my dad out because he was always getting into
political arguments with her because he liked President Truman and she didn't. I
think perhaps my dad was some sort of aide to President Truman, because he liked him
so much. Most probably he was out of the country during the war when I was growing
up on some sort of mission. I think he was the kind of guy who would fight for his
country and what was right. Maybe he got killed fighting the Nazis and he's with
God now and that's how come he never managed to find me.

    I like President Truman, the way Dad would of wanted me to. He dropped the
atom bomb on Japan and saved millions of lives because if he hadn't of, then there
would of been a lot more war than there was and more people would of been killed.
I think it was a good thing to drop the atomic bomb on Japan.

    That is all I have to say about my parents.

Charlton Home

DREAM, 5/27/63

" A man was in my old house, with my mom. They were eating some stuff like raw dough, and my mom choked on a piece. The guy with her tried to fish it out of her throat. He got his whole hand in her mouth and then it was like he had his whole arm down her throat. He told me to get a doctor, so I ran out of the room but the house was all different and there wasn't any doctor there anyway, so I went back to find mom. I was walking down this sort of hallway, and it was dark and I saw what looked like my mom and this guy dancing, old fashioned dancing at the other end of the room, and they didn't have any clothes on. They were sort of clopping around like a horse in a pantomine with two guys in a suit. When they got nearer, I saw they weren't dancing at all, they were squashed together like siamese twins, joined at the face and chest and stomach. They didn't have any face, you could only see their ears, two on either side of the head facing towards each other. Their hands were growing into each other as well, but they had all four legs free and they were sort of dancing sideways towards me down the dark hall like a crab, and there was something tripping 'em up, wrapped around their feet, and I looked down and I saw it was trousers and underwear and stuff. They were coming towards me, and then I woke up. I had feelings when I woke up. Dirty feelings, thoughts and stuff. The dream it sort of upset me, physically. I couldn't help it. I feel bad just talking about it."

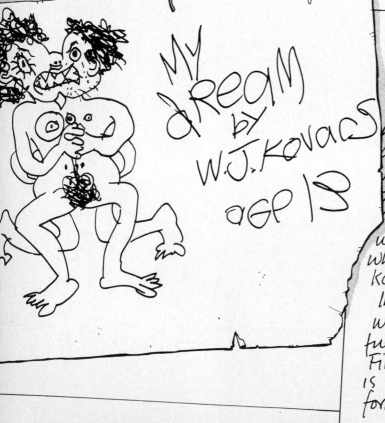

From the desk of: Dr. Malcolm

10/

Walter Joseph Kovacs promises to a complex case, especially in of the extreme nature of hi vigilante activities. It may possible to identify a new syndrome that will help us understand those other people who have in the past shared Kovacs masked vigilante activi In any event, keep notes with an eye to possible future publication.
First interview with Kovacs is Friday afternoon. lookin forward to it.

1

OH!

HA.

O-KAAY...

NOW WHERE'S THE *DASH LIGHTER*?

AHH.

YEEEEE!

2

A BROTHER TO DRAGONS

YEAH, WELL, AT LEAST YOU WERE LIVING OUT YOUR *OWN* FANTASIES. I WAS LIVING OUT MY *MOTHER'S.*

Y'KNOW, I'M REALLY *IMPRESSED* BY ALL THIS *EQUIPMENT.* IT MUST HAVE COST YOU A *FORTUNE.*

WHAT'S THIS *CABINET* OVER HERE?

OH, THAT'S JUST *SOUVENIRS* AND JUNK LIKE THAT.

AS FOR THE *MONEY,* MY DAD WAS IN *BANKING.* HE LEFT ME A LOT OF MONEY WHEN HE *DIED.*

I WAS ALWAYS KIND OF *SURPRISED* ABOUT THAT.

I MEAN, HE ALWAYS SEEMED *DISAPPOINTED* IN ME. HE WANTED ME TO FOLLOW HIM INTO *BANKING,* BUT I WAS JUST INTERESTED IN *BIRDS* AND *AIRPLANES* AND *MYTHOLOGY.* YOU KNOW. *KID'S* STUFF.

HMM. WHAT'S *THIS*?

THAT? OH, *THAT* ISN'T ANYBODY. IT'S JUST THIS *VICE QUEEN* I PUT AWAY BACK IN '68. CALLED HERSELF *DUSK WOMAN* OR SOMETHING.

"THE *TWILIGHT LADY*"

SHE SENT YOU HER PICTURE?

From one 'Night Bird' to Another. Love from The Twilight Lady

YEAH, WELL, I GUESS SHE HAD SORT OF A *FIXATION.* SHE WAS A *VERY* SICK WOMAN.

I KEEP MEANING TO THROW THAT PICTURE *AWAY,* BUT YOU KNOW HOW IT *IS*...

MMM.

I SEE YOU HAVE A LOT OF PICTURES OF *BIRDS* AND STUFF. THAT WAS *MY* FANTASY, WHEN I WAS A *KID*: TO WORK WITH *ANIMALS* ...

I JUST LIKED *BIRDS,* MOSTLY. JUST THE IDEA OF *FLYING* ...

AS A KID, I READ ABOUT *PEGASUS,* FLYING *CARPETS,* THEN LATER ABOUT *BIRDS* AND *PLANES.*

FINALLY, I *MASTERED* IN AERONAUTICS AND ZOOLOGY AT *HARVARD.*

GUESS IT HELPED ME DESIGN THIS *JALOPY* HERE.

JALOPY? *THAT'S* A WORD I HAVEN'T HEARD IN A LONG TIME.

HEH. I PROBABLY PICKED IT UP FROM *HOLLIS.*

HOLLIS WAS SOMETHING *ELSE* THAT INFLUENCED ME AS A KID. I *IDOLIZED* HIM...

...BUT THEN I GUESS THAT'S PRETTY *OBVIOUS.*

WELCOME *ABOARD.* YOU WANT TO TAKE A LOOK *AROUND* WHILE I FINISH CHECKING THE *SHIP* OUT?

SURE. AND DON'T *WORRY* ... I WON'T *TOUCH* ANYTHING.

5

I MEAN, LOOK AT RORSCHACH, THE CONDITION HE'S IN. HE WAS NORMAL ONCE.

SURE, HE WAS QUIET, HE WAS GRIM, BUT HE STILL HAD ALL THE BUTTONS ON HIS OVERCOAT.

SOON AFTER I STARTED OUT, WE BLITZED THE BIG FIGURE TOGETHER. TACTICALLY, RORSCHACH WAS BRILLIANT. HE WAS SO UNPREDICTABLE.

WHAT I'M SAYING IS, HE WAS RATIONAL THEN.

OVER THE YEARS, THAT MASK'S EATEN HIS BRAINS.

WASN'T ANYTHING GOOD ABOUT THOSE YEARS? I MEAN, ALL THESE GADGETS YOU DESIGNED... IF THAT WAS ME, I'D FEEL PROUD.

YOU'RE REALLY INTERESTED IN ALL THIS STUFF?

WELL, UH, DID I SHOW YOU MY GOGGLES?

I MEAN, IF YOU LIKE THIS SORT OF GARBAGE... I GUESS IT'S PRETTY KITSCH OR CAMP OR WHATEVER...

DAN, DON'T BE SO SELF-DEPRECATING. I WAS ADMIRING THE GOGGLES EARLIER.

THOSE LENSES ARE PRETTY DUSTY...

HMM. THEY WORK BEST IN DARKNESS, SO I'LL KILL THE LIGHTS. I'VE GOT THIS LITTLE CONSOLE IN MY BELT HERE...

WHAT ELSE HAVE YOU GOT IN THERE? CHOCOLATE RATIONS? BOY SCOUT KNIFE? ARMY ISSUE CONTRACEPTIVES?

HA HA HA HA. NO, IT'S MOSTLY PRETTY BORING... RESPIRATOR MASKS, SMOKE BOMBS, FINGERPRINT KIT, POCKET LASER, THIS LITTLE CONSOLE...

YOU KNOW.

THE USUAL STUFF.

OKAY, NOW IF I SNUFF THE LIGHTS IN THE SHIP'S CABIN AND IN THE KITCHEN UPSTAIRS...

HA! SHOW-OFF.

HEY, WHAT ARE THESE GOGGLES SUPPOSED TO DO? I CAN'T SEE ANYTHING. ARE THEY BROKEN?

NO. YOU JUST PRESS HERE TO ROTATE THE LENSES A QUARTER TURN, LIKE THIS.

AS I REMEMBER, THEY WORK PRETTY GOOD. NO MATTER HOW BLACK IT GOT, WHEN I LOOKED THROUGH THESE GOGGLES...

...EVERYTHING WAS CLEAR AS DAY.

OOOOH!

9

DAN, THIS IS *FABULOUS*. THIS MUST BE WHAT IT'S LIKE HAVING *POWERS*...Y'KNOW, SPECIAL VISION AND LIKE THAT.

IT MUST BE SO STRANGE BEING *JON*. *HE* CAN SEE *NEUTRINOS*...

HM. WELL, IT'S GETTING *LATE*...

OH, OKAY. I'M ALL THROUGH *PLAYING* WITH THEM, ANYWAY.

...THOUGH MAYBE I'LL BORROW THEM FOR *PALE HORSE'S* MADISON SQUARE GARDEN CONCERTS IN EARLY *NOVEMBER*. THEY'RE KINDA *DEVO*.

DEVO?

JUST A SECOND... LET'S PUT THE LIGHTS ON UP-STAIRS.

SURE. DEVO. *"ARE WE NOT MEN?"* BAND FROM *OHIO*. LATE *SEVENTIES*.

OH. WELL, I'M MOSTLY INTO BILLIE HOLIDAY, NELLIE LUTCHER, LOUIS JORDAN,... STUFF LIKE THAT.

DO YOU MISS JON?

JON? NO... ALTHOUGH I KEEP THINKING I *SHOULD*.

BUT, YOU SEE, EVEN WHEN I WAS *WITH* HIM, HE WAS NEVER REALLY *THERE*. THERE WAS NO REAL HUMAN *CONTACT*; NO *PHYSICAL* CONTACT...

I WAS SO *LONELY*...

YES. I KNOW. LAURIE SOMETIMES I'VE FELT...

...AND, LIKE, IT WASN'T JUST THE *ISOLATION*. I USED TO WORK OUT IN A *GYM* A LOT AS A KID, ALL BY MYSELF, SO BEING *ALONE'S* NO BIG DEAL.

I MEAN, TAKE *YOU*, FOR EXAMPLE. YOU *LIKE* LIVING HERE ON YOUR OWN, SO...

DAN? WHAT ARE YOU *DOING*?

UHH, NOTHING. JUST TRYING TO KEEP THESE LICKS OF HAIR IN *FRONT* TIDY. PLEASE ...CARRY ON.

WELL, WHAT I'M *SAYING* IS THAT AT *ROCKEFELLER* I GOT THE *BAD* SIDE OF ISOLATION WITHOUT THE *COMPENSATIONS*, LIKE *PRIVACY*.

THERE WAS NOBODY TO *TALK* TO, BUT I'D ALWAYS FEEL LIKE I WAS UNDER *OBSERVATION*.

HMM.

IT MUST BE GREAT FOR YOU, HAVING A *SECRET IDENTITY*, A SECRET *PLACE* NOBODY *KNOWS* ABOUT.

YOU CAN JUST COME DOWN HERE TO HANG OUT AND THERE'S NOBODY CHECKING *UP* ON YOU...

NOBODY *WATCHING* YOU.

ISN'T THERE?

THESE DAYS, I FEEL LIKE SOMETHING'S WATCHING MY EVERY *MOVE*.

10

DAN, YOU SOUND LIKE 'RORSCHACH'. THIS 'MASK KILLER' THING, IT DOESN'T HOLD UP.

WHERE'S THE CONSPIRACY?

I MEAN, JON LEFT EARTH OF HIS OWN FREE WILL; RORSCHACH WAS CAUGHT RED-HANDED COMMITTING MURDER, FOR GOD'S SAKE...

I WASN'T REALLY THINKING ABOUT THE MASK KILLER, BUT...

I DON'T KNOW. THAT RORSCHACH MURDER THING SOUNDED FUNNY. HE WOULDN'T JUST SHOOT SOMEBODY. IT'S TOO ORDINARY.

ANYWAY, IT'S ALMOST SIX O'CLOCK NEWS TIME. WANT COFFEE?

SURE. BLACK AS THE DEVIL AND SWEET AS A STOLEN KISS.

WHAT?

NO MILK: TWO SUGARS. POLISH FOLK SAYING. OH, INCIDENTALLY, DID YOU SEE THAT PACKAGE THAT ARRIVED FOR ME?

UH, NO. I DIDN'T.

JUST MY CLOTHES, FORWARDED FROM ROCKEFELLER. MY OLD COSTUME, STUFF LIKE THAT.

OH, YEAH, AND A LETTER TELLING ME I DON'T HAVE CANCER. HOPE YOU DON'T MIND ME USING YOUR ADDRESS.

LONG AS YOU LIKE. SEE, I'M NOT REALLY THAT SOLITARY BY INCLINATION.

WELL, I JUST DON'T WANT TO GET IN THE WAY OF YOUR WORK OR ANYTHING.

WHAT IS IT THAT YOU DO, ACTUALLY?

OH, WELL, Y'KNOW. NOT A LOT, I GUESS. I SOMETIMES WRITE PIECES FOR ORNITHOLOGICAL JOURNALS.

REALLY? YOU DO A LOT OF THAT?

..., LATEST IN A SERIES OF TENEMENT FIRES ALLEGEDLY DESIGNED TO REMOVE SITTING TENANTS...

NO. NOT MUCH. I HAVEN'T WRITTEN ANYTHING SINCE LAST APRIL. MOST PEOPLE FIND IT ALL PRETTY BORING, I GUESS...

...MEANWHILE, INVESTIGATIONS INTO CAPTURED VIGILANTE RORSCHACH ARE CONTINUING...

USUALLY, AS SOON AS I MENTION ORNITHOLOGY, FOLKS SORT OF SWITCH OFF AND...

SHHHH!

TODAY, POLICE ALLOWED NEWS CAMERAMEN INTO THE APARTMENT USED BY RORSCHACH, REAL NAME WALTER JOSEPH KOVACS.

HIS LANDLADY, MS. DOLORES SHAIRP, DESCRIBED KOVACS AS 'A NAZI PERVERT' AND SAID THAT HE'D FREQUENTLY PROPOSITIONED HER SEXUALLY...

HA! I KNEW IT!

SHE POINTED OUT STACKS OF RIGHT WING LITERATURE INCLUDING BACK ISSUES OF THE NEW FRONTIERSMAN.

11

16

UHHMN. JON..?

DID YOU SHUB UBBUH NUHNUHDUH ...

MMM.

UH, DAN?

I'M READY.

ME TOO.

LET'S GO.

UH, WILL THIS THING STILL *FLY* OKAY AND EVERYTHING?

SURE. I RAN A SCAN ON ARCHIE EARLIER: NOT A FEATHER OUT OF PLACE. LET ME JUST PLUG THE STEERING COLUMN IN OVER *HERE*...

HMM. GOT *SOOT* IN HIS EYES...

OH! WE'RE *MOVING*.

YES. I'M SORRY...HE ALWAYS GIVES THAT LITTLE *LURCH* WHEN HE STARTS UP. CAN'T SEEM TO IRON IT OUT.

BETTER WASH THESE WINDOWS DOWN BEFORE WE HIT THE *EXIT* TUNNEL...

WOW. IT'S LIKE BEING ON A *GHOST TRAIN*: THE DOORS BUMP *OPEN*, YOU ENTER THE *TUNNEL*...

HEH. ACTUALLY, IT'S A FORGOTTEN SECTION OF *SUBWAY* I CONVERTED AFTER BUYING THE BUILDING *ABOVE*.

LET'S PICK UP A LITTLE *SPEED* HERE.

IS IT OKAY TO *GO* THIS FAST? WHERE DOES THE TUNNEL COME *OUT*?

A DERELICT *WAREHOUSE* TWO BLOCKS *NORTH*. I OWN THAT, TOO. LET'S JUST HOPE THE STEEL *FLOOD DOORS* OVER THE END OF THE *TUNNEL* HAVEN'T *RUSTED SHUT*.

RUSTED *SHUT*? *DAN!* ARE YOU...?

RELAX. JUST KIDDING. OKAY, IN A MOMENT I'M GOING TO TAKE HIM *UP* JUST HAVE TO ARRANGE SOME *CLOUD COVER* WITH THE *FOG-SCREENS*...

FOG-SCREENS?

DRY ICE. ARCHIE BREATHES *SMOKE* AS WELL AS *FIRE*.

OKAY NOW, HOLD *TIGHT*. I'M ROLLING BACK THE WAREHOUSE ROOF.

HERE WE *GO*...

22

OKAY, THERE'S *WATER CANNONS* TRAINED ON THE *LOWER STORYS* TO SLOW DOWN THE *FIRE.*

ALL YOU *PEOPLE* IN THERE, PLEASE GET TO THE *TOP FLOOR.* WE'LL JOIN YOU IN A *MOMENT.*

THANK YOU.

I'LL EXTEND A *RAMP* FROM THE *REAR DOOR* TO A *WINDOW,* SO WE CAN SHEPHERD EVERYBODY ONTO THE *SHIP.*

HMM. IF I'M GOING TO BE WORKING CLOSE TO THE *BLAZE,* I WON'T NEED MY *COAT.*

WELL?

UH?

WUH, WELL *WHAT?*

WELL WHAT ABOUT THE *RAMP?* THERE'S A BUNCH OF PEOPLE STILL NEED THEIR *ASSES* HAULED OUT OF THE FIRE, REMEMBER?

OH. OH, RIGHT. SURE...

THE RAMP. ABSOLUTELY...

GET *BACK!* IT'S *POKIN'* SOMETHIN' AT THE BUILDING!

MOM? THAT GUY IN THE *SPACE ROCKET,* IS THAT *JESUS?*

24

I am a brother to dragons,
and a companion to owls.
My skin is black upon me,
and my bones are burned with heat.

JOB chapter 30, verses 29-30

The following text is reprinted from the Journal of The American Ornithological Society, Fall 1983.

BLOOD·FROM·THE
SHOULDER·OF·PALLAS

□□□□□□□□□ BY DANIEL DREIBERG □□□□□□□□□

Is it possible, I wonder, to study a bird so closely, to observe and catalogue its peculiarities in such minute detail, that it becomes invisible? Is it possible that while fastidiously calibrating the span of its wings or the length of its tarsus, we somehow lose sight of its poetry? That in our pedestrian descriptions of a marbled or vermiculated plumage we forfeit a glimpse of living canvases, cascades of carefully toned browns and golds that would shame Kandinsky, misty explosions of color to rival Monet? I believe that we do. I believe that in approaching our subject with the sensibilities of statisticians and dissectionists, we distance ourselves increasingly from the marvelous and spell-binding planet of imagination whose gravity drew us to our studies in the first place.

This is not to say that we should cease to establish facts and to verify our information, but merely to suggest that unless those facts can be imbued with the flash of poetic insight then they remain dull gems; semi-precious stones scarcely worth the collecting.

When we stare into the catatonic black bead of a Parakeet's eye we must teach ourselves to glimpse the cold, alien madness that Max Ernst perceived when he chose to robe his naked brides in confections of scarlet feather and the transplanted monstrous heads of exotic birds. When some ocean-going Kite or Tern is captured in the sharp blue gaze of our Zeiss lenses, we must be able to see the stop motion flight of sepia gulls through the early kinetic photographs of Muybridge, beating white wings tracing a slow oscilloscope line through space and time.

Looking at a hawk, we see the minute differences in width of the shaft lines on the underfeathers where the Egyptians once saw Horus and the burning eye of holy vengeance incarnate. Until we transform our mere sightings into genuine visions; until our ear is mature enough to order a symphony from the shrill pandemonium of the aviary; until then we may have a hobby, but we shall not have a passion.

When I was a boy, my passion was for owls. During the long summers of the early fifties, while the rest of the country was apparently watching the skies for incoming flying saucers or Soviet missiles, I would hare across the New England fields in the heart of the night, sneakers munching through the dried grass and bracken towards my watch, where I would sit peering upwards in hope of a different sort of spectacle, ears straining for the weird scream that meant an old bird was out combing the dark for sustenance, a mad hermit screech, glaringly distinct from the snoring hiss of a younger owl.

Somewhere over the years; sometime during the yawning expanse between those snug years in the afterglow of a war well won and these current times, huddled in the looming shadow of a war unwinnable; someplace along the line my passion got lost, unwittingly refined from the original gleaming ore down to a banal and lusterless filing system. This gradual tarnishing had gone unnoticed, unchecked, finally calcifying into unthinking habit. It was not until comparatively recently that I managed to catch a dazzling glimpse of the motherlode through the accumulated dust of methodical study and academia: visiting a sick acquaintance at a hospital in Maine on behalf of a mutual friend, walking back across the shadowy parking lot with my mind reduced to blankness by the various concerns of the day, I suddenly and unexpectedly heard the cry of a hunting owl.

It was a bird advanced in years, its shriek that of a deranged old man, wheeling madly through the dark and freezing sky against the ragged night clouds, and the sound halted me in my footsteps. It is a fallacy to suppose that owls screech to startle their prey from hiding, as some have suggested; the cry of the hunting owl is a voice from Hell, and it turns the scrabbling voles to statues, roots the weasel to the soil. In my instant of paralysis there on the glistening macadam, between the sleeping automobiles, I understood the purpose behind the cry with a biting clarity, the way I'd understood it as a boy, belly flat against the warm summer earth. In that extended and timeless moment, I felt the kinship of simple animal fear along with all those other creatures much smaller and more vulnerable than I who had heard the scream as I had heard it, were struck motionless as I was. The owl was not attempting to frighten his food into revealing itself. Perched with disconcerting stillness upon its branch for hours, drinking in the darkness through dilated and thirsty pupils, the owl had already spotted its dinner. The screech served merely to transfix the chosen morsel, pinning it to the ground with a shrill nail of blind, helpless terror. Not knowing which of us had been selected, I stood frozen along with the rodents of the field, my heart hammering as it waited for the sudden clutch of sharpened steel fingers that would provide my first and only indication that I was the predetermined victim. The feathers of owls are soft and downy; they make no sound at all as they drop through the dark stratas of the sky. The silence before an owl swoops is a V-Bomb silence, and you never hear the one that hits you.

Somewhere away in the crepuscular gloom beyond the yellow-lit hospital grounds I thought I heard something small emit its ultimate squeal. The moment had passed. I could move again, along with all the relieved, invisible denizens of the tall grass. We were safe. It wasn't screaming for us, not this time. We could continue with our nocturnal business, with our lives, searching for a meal or a mate. We were not twitching nervelessly in stifling, stinking darkness, head first down the gullet of the swooping horror, our tails dangling pathetically from that vicious scimitar beak for hours before finally our hind legs and pelvic girdle are disgorged, our empty, matted skin curiously inverted by the process.

Although I had recovered my motor abilities in the aftermath of the owl's shriek, I found that my equilibrium was not so easily regained. Some facet of the experience had struck a chord in me, forged a connection between my dulled and jaded adult self and the child who sprawled in faint starlight while the great night hunters staged dramas full of hunger and death in the opaque jet air above me. An urge to experience rather than merely record had been rekindled within me, prompting the thought processes, the self-evaluation that has led to this current article.

As I remarked earlier, this is not to suggest that I immediately foreswore all academic endeavor and research pertaining to the field in order to run away and eke out some naked and primordial existence in the woods. Quite the contrary: I hurled myself into the study of my subject with renewed fervor, able to see the dry facts and arid descriptions in the same transforming magical light that had favored them when I was younger. A scientific understanding of the beautifully synchronized and articulated motion of an owl's individual feathers during flight does not impede a poetic appreciation of the same phenomenon. Rather, the two enhance each other, a more lyrical eye lending the cold data a romance from which it has long been divorced.

Immersing myself avidly in dusty and long untouched reference books I came across forgotten passages that would make me almost breathless, dreary-looking tomes that would reveal themselves to be treasure houses of iridescent wonder. I rediscovered many long-lost gems amongst the cobwebs, antique and functional stretches of descriptive prose which nonetheless conveyed the violent and terrible essence of their subject matter effortlessly.

I stumbled once more across T.A. Coward's engrossing account on an encounter with an Eagle Owl: "In Norway I saw a bird that had been taken when in down from the nest, but it not only assumed the typical terrifying attitude, but made frequent dashes at the wire, striking with its feet. It puffed its feathers out, framed its head in its wings, and fired off a volley of loud cracks from its snapping beak, but what struck me most was the scintillating flash of its great orange eyes."

Then of course there is Hudson's account of the Magellanic Eagle-Owl which he wounded in Patagonia: "The irides were of a bright orange color, but every time I attempted to approach the bird they kindled into great globes of quivering yellow flame, the black pupils being surrounded by a scintillating crimson light which threw out minute yellow sparks into the air." In long-buried words such as the foregoing I caught some of the searing, apocalyptic intensity that I had felt in that wet hospital parking lot in Maine.

Nowadays, when I observe some specimen of *Carine noctua*, I try to look past the fine grey down on the toes, to see beyond the white spots arranged in neat lines, like a firework display across its brow. Instead, I try to see the bird whose image the Greeks carved into their coins, sitting patiently at the ear of the Goddess Pallas Athene, silently sharing her immortal wisdom.

Perhaps, instead of measuring the feathered tufts surmounting its ears, we should speculate on what those ears may have heard. Perhaps when considering the manner in which it grips its branch, with two toes in front and the reversible outer toe clutching from behind, we should allow ourselves to pause for a moment, and acknowledge that these same claws must once have drawn blood from the shoulder of Pallas.

OLD GHOSTS

Panel 1: IT'S LIKE ALL OUR OLD NIGHTMARES COME BACK TO HAUNT US, Y'KNOW?

ADRIFT AND STARVING, MY DARKEST IMAGININGS WELLED UP UNCHECKED, SPILLING FROM BRAIN TO HEART LIKE BLACK INK, IMPOSSIBLE TO REMOVE

Panel 2: RED INVASIONS, MASKED MEN... SEEN THIS WEEK'S NOVA EXPRESS? "SPIRIT OF '77". I MEAN, I REMEMBER 1977...

GOD SPARE US.

I PICTURED DAVIDSTOWN'S QUIET STREETS OVERRUN BY TATTOOED FIENDS. RECALLING THEIR BRUTALITY, I MOANED.

Panel 3: EVERYTHING'S GOING TO HELL. I'M JUST GLAD MY ROSA AIN'T ALIVE TO SEE.

THE FREIGHTER HAD SURELY REACHED DAVIDSTOWN ALREADY. MY WIFE WAS ALMOST CERTAINLY DEAD. THESE NOTIONS TRANSFIXED ME, STOPPING TIME IN ITS TRACKS.

Panel 4: TODAY WOULDA BEEN OUR ANNIVERSARY. SUNDAY, 27TH OCTOBER. FUNNY, THIS TIME O'YEAR SHE'S ALWAYS ON MY MIND.

I REMEMBERED HER WAVING GOODBYE FROM THE VERANDAH SHADOWS, SUNLIGHT ILLUMINATING ONE CHEEK BONE.

DEAD?

Panel 5: SHE'DA HATED HOW THIS SUPERHERO THING TURNED OUT: DOC MANHATTAN EXILED, OZYMANDIAS SHOT AT...

...AN' RORSCHACH! SEE INNA GAZETTE HE ATTACKED SOME OTHER PRISONER WITH HOT FAT? JESUS.

THOSE GLORIOUS DAYS; THAT INNOCENCE...

DEAD?

Panel 6: I STILL CAN'T BELIEVE IT...HIM COMIN' HERE EVERY DAY, NOBODY REALIZIN'. STILL, THAT'S LIFE: LOTTA STUFF HAPPENS UNDER THE WATERLINE...

DEAD: I IMAGINED MY SHIPMATES' BLOATED CORPSES, CARRYING MY RAFT ON FISHEATEN BACKS...

Panel 7: IN FACT...OH, GAZETTE? SURE. HEY, SEE THIS RORSCHACH ITEM? HE WAS A CUSTOMER HERE. ALWAYS KINDA SUSPECTED, BUT, HEY, PRETTY INCREDIBLE, RIGHT?

KOVACS...? UH, YES. INCREDIBLE. THANK YOU.

New York Gazette

DEAD: THE PUTREFYING SHARK, ITS SNARL NO LONGER CONVINCING...

Panel 8: BYE. HAVE A NICE DAY.

DEAD: I HEAR HER PLEADING; SEE THEIR YELLOWED SMILES, THEIR CUTLASSES CARVING RELENTLESSLY UNTIL ALL HER PERSONALITY, ALL HER SUBTLETIES OF POSTURE AND EXPRESSION ARE OBLITERATED, REDUCED TO MEAT...

DEAD.

Panel 9: HMM. PREOCCUPIED TYPE. PROBABLY A TEACHER, THINKIN' ABOUT ALGEBRA, RELATIVITY, WHATEVER. WHADDA THOSE GUYS KNOW ABOUT LIFE? WORLD'S GOING CRAZY, THEY DON'T EVEN NOTICE!

FINALLY, FACED WITH HORRORS BOTH INTOLERABLE AND UNAVOIDABLE, I CHOSE MADNESS.

3

THIS IS INSANITY.

WE'RE YOUNG *LOVERS*, THE WORLD COULD END *TOMORROW* AND HOW ARE WE SPENDING SUNDAY *EVENING*? WE'RE PLANNING TO BUST A *HOMICIDAL MANIAC* OUT OF SING-SING!

LISTEN, I'LL LOAD THOSE *HOVER BIKES* AFTER THIS *CIGARETTE*, OKAY?

SURE.

AND IT'S NOT INSANITY. *SOMETHING'S* GOING ON: FOUR ADVENTURERS ATTACKED WITHIN ELEVEN DAYS ISN'T COINCIDENCE.

MAYBE THAT CANCER-SCARE *MEDIA ASSAULT* THAT PROMPTED JON'S *EXILE* WAS PART OF SOMEBODY'S *PLAN*. MAYBE SOMEONE *INTENDED* TO START WORLD WAR THREE.

OH DAN, COME ON...

LAURIE, YOU *LIVED* WITH JON. *YOU* DIDN'T CONTRACT *CANCER* FROM HIM. MAYBE *NOBODY* DID.

MY COMPUTER LISTS MOST PEOPLE *NOVA EXPRESS* MENTIONED AS EMPLOYED BY A *RESEARCH COMPANY* CALLED "DIMENSIONAL DEVELOPMENTS" BETWEEN '67 AND '85. WEIRD, HUH?

JANEY *SLATER*, WALLY *WEAVER*... THEY EVEN GAVE *MOLOCH* A TEMPORARY JOB WHEN HE LEFT PRISON.

THEY FUND THE *INSTITUTE FOR EXTRASPATIAL STUDIES*; ANOTHER COMPANY, *PYRAMID DELIVERIES*, FUNDS *THEM*. THIS *CORPORATE STRUCTURE* STUFF'S A *MAZE*...

YEAH? WELL THAT AND YOUR LOGIC *BOTH*. I MEAN, *WHY* RISK SPRINGING A *LIABILITY* LIKE RORSCHACH? WE TOOK *ENOUGH* CHANCES WITH THAT *TENEMENT RESCUE*.

RORSCHACH'S BEEN INVESTIGATING THIS THING ALL *ALONG*. WE NEED HIS *INFORMATION*.

...AND WE MAY NOT HAVE LONG TO *GET* IT. TODAY'S *GAZETTE* MENTIONS *DEATH THREATS* FOLLOWING YESTERDAY'S *HOT FAT INCIDENT*.

IT'S *IMPORTANT*, LAURIE. IF JON'S *EXILE* AND ITS *CONSEQUENCES* WERE *PREMEDITATED*, MAYBE IT'S THE MOST IMPORTANT THING IN THE *WORLD*.

REDS CROSS PAKISTAN BORDER

4

SUPERHERO SAVES *WORLD*, HUH? THIS IS SOME ELABORATE *SCAM* TO GET ME BACK INTO MY *COSTUME*, RIGHT?

HA HA. LAURIE, THE COSTUME WAS *YOUR* IDEA...

WHAAAT? THAT'S *RIDICULOUS!* I *LOATHE* THAT HALLOWEEN SUIT. *OBVIOUSLY,* I WORE IT TO HELP *YOU.*

OH, *OBVIOUSLY.*

OWN *UP,* LAURIE: DOESN'T THIS BRING ALL THOSE OLD TIMES FLOODING BACK? *NIGHT* PATROLS; HAVING A *SECRET...*

WELLL... YEAH, *PATROLS* WERE OKAY. I HAD NINE DIFFERENT *ROUTES* OVER WASHINGTON'S ROOFTOPS. ROUTE *FIVE* WAS BEST.

Panel 3:

THAT HAD THE *WHITE HOUSE,* THE *LINCOLN MEMORIAL* AND THEN *HOME* TO ME AND JON'S FABULOUS *APARTMENT.* WE WERE *HAPPY* THERE. WE...

OH *DAN,* I'M *SORRY.* I KEEP MENTIONING *JON.* HE JUST *POPS UP* WHEN I DON'T *EXPECT* IT.

Panel 4:

DON'T WORRY. IT'S EARLY DAYS. A FEW *SKELETONS* ARE BOUND TO KEEP JUMPING OUT OF THE CLOSET.

I WAS JUST THINKING ABOUT *ADRIAN.* WE OUGHT TO *CONTACT* HIM, BUT MAYBE NOT TILL *AFTER* THE *JAILBREAK.*

Panel 5:

I MEAN, IN *HIS* POSITION, KNOWING *BEFORE-HAND* WOULD BE *COMPROMISING.* HE MIGHT FEEL OBLIGED TO *STOP* US.

DAN, SOME-TIMES, *I* FEEL OBLIGED TO STOP US. I MEAN, A *JAILBREAK.* I CAN'T BELIEVE WE'RE TAKING THIS *SERIOUSLY.*

ASSUMING SOMEBODY'S USING *JON* TO TRIGGER *ARMAGEDDON,* THEN HOW *SHOULD* WE TAKE IT? IT'S *SERIOUS...*

...AND FOR *RORSCHACH,* IF THE MOOD AROUND THAT PRISON GETS ANY *UGLIER,* IT'S A MATTER OF LIFE OR *DEATH.*

5

EXCUSE ME? MY NAME'S DETECTIVE STEVEN *FINE*, I'M LOOKING FOR A DANIEL *DREIBERG*.

I'M DAN DREIBERG.

UH, YOU BETTER COME *IN*...

ALMOST *THROUGH* HERE, MR. DREIBERG. THIS BABY'LL HOLD OFF AN *ARMY*. SORRY WE KEPT YOU *WAITING* FOR THE *INSTALLATION*.

THAT'S OKAY. WELL, DETECTIVE, HOW CAN I *HELP* YOU?

EDWARD *BLAKE*. HOMICIDE VICTIM. YOU *KNEW* HIM.

UH. YES. VAGUELY.

YOU KNEW HIM WELL ENOUGH TO ATTEND HIS *FUNERAL*. I SAW THE *PHOTOGRAPHS*: YOU, ADRIAN *VEIDT*, DOC *MANHATTAN*.

YOU KEEP HEAVY COMPANY, MR. DREIBERG.

I MET BLAKE THROUGH *VEIDT*. I, UH, ONCE DONATED SOME *MONEY* TO ONE OF VEIDT'S *CHARITIES*.

UH-HUH.

BIG *GUY*, THAT *BLAKE*. FOR A DIPLOMAT. QUITE A *HEROIC* FIGURE. MAYBE HE WORKED *OUT*, HUH?

FUNNY... THERE'S BEEN A *LOT* OF "HEROIC FIGURES" IN THE NEWS LATELY: *RORSCHACH* CAPTURED, *VEIDT* SHOT AT, DOC *MANHATTAN* LEAVES *EARTH*, DAMN NEAR KICKING OFF WORLD WAR *THREE*...

CIGARETTE, MR. *DREIBERG*?

NO. THANKS. I DON'T.

VERY WISE.

... AND THEN THERE WAS THAT THING LAST *WEEKEND*. YOU *READ* ABOUT THAT? THAT *TENEMENT FIRE*?

ALL *FINISHED*, MR. DREIBERG. YOU GOT MAXIMUM *SECURITY*.

New York Ga
TANKS MASS I EASTERN EURO
'PURELY DEFENSIVE' SAY REDS.
CALIFORNIA: GOVE REAGAN URGES HARD LINE

GORDIAN KNOT

UH, *RIGHT*. RIGHT, *THANKS*! I'LL SETTLE BY *CHECK*...

CRAZIEST STORY... THIS *AIRSHIP* RESCUES ALL THESE *PEOPLE*, HOVERING DOWN BETWEEN THE *BUILDINGS*. AIN'T MANY AIRSHIPS CAN DO *THAT*.

NO?

NO. INTERVIEWED SOME WITNESSES, BUT THE *DETAILS* WERE GARBLED: PILOT WORE *GOGGLES*; HAD A FEMALE *ACCOMPLICE*; PLAYED *MUSIC*; SERVED *COFFEE*...

HEY... "SWEET CHARIOT" *SUGAR CUBES*! ONLY COME IN *CATERING* PACKS, RIGHT?

UH, YES. I BELIEVE SO. WHY?

SWEET CHAR "SUGAR CATERING PACK

NO REASON.

Y'KNOW, THE ONLY SHIP I EVER HEARD OF COULD MANEUVER BETWEEN *BUILDINGS* BELONGED TO ONE OF THOSE MASKED *ADVENTURERS* THEY OUTLAWED IN '77.

COULDN'T HAVE *BEEN* HIM, NATURALLY... HE'D BE IN HIS *FORTIES* NOW.

8

I MEAN, GUYS THAT AGE LIKE *US*, WE'RE *UNHEALTHY*. WE GET UP IN THE MORNING AND COUGH OUR *LUNGS* UP, WE...

...OH, BUT THEN I FORGOT. YOU DON'T *SMOKE*, DO YOU?

NO. LISTEN, WHAT'S THIS *ABOUT*?

AIN'T ABOUT NOTHING. I'M NOT EVEN ON *DUTY*. JUST CALLED TO SEE IF YOU KNEW ANYTHING ABOUT *BLAKE*.

I'M AFRAID *NOT*. WE WEREN'T *CLOSE*.

UH, THAT LEADS TO THE *LUMBER ROOM*. KEY'S LOST, I'M AFRAID.

Panel 3:
NO SWEAT. I GOTTA GO, ANYWAY. SAY, I NOTICED THIS CALENDAR *EARLIER*. NICE *OWL*.

Y'KNOW, TWO KINDS OF PEOPLE HAVE *CALENDARS*: PEOPLE WHO PEEK AT NEXT MONTH'S PICTURE IN *ADVANCE* AND PEOPLE WHO *DON'T*. WHICH ARE YOU?

I *DON'T*.

Panel 4:
YOU OUGHTTA. IT PAYS TO LOOK AHEAD.

HMM. *NOVEMBER'S* A *HAWK* TAKING A *SPARROW* IN *FLIGHT*. OMINOUS KINDA *PICTURE*, HUH?

AW HELL... I HOPE I DIDN'T SPOIL THE *SURPRISE* FOR YOU?

Panel 5:
OH, DON'T WORRY. LIFE HAS ENOUGH SURPRISES.

I'LL BET. INCIDENTALLY, I'M SORRY FOR BORING YOU WITH THAT TALK ABOUT *ADVENTURERS*. IT'S A KINDA *HOBBY HORSE* OF MINE.

SINCE I ARRESTED *RORSCHACH*, THEY'VE BEEN PREYING ON MY MIND.

NOVEMBER
T W T F
1 2
7 8 9
14 15 1
21 22 23 24
8 29 30

I MEAN, RESCUING *FIRE* VICTIMS, NOBODY CONDEMNS *THAT*, BUT IF IT WENT ANY *FURTHER*... IT'S LIKE NOVA EXPRESS OF '77 *SAYS*: "*SPIRIT OF '77*". BRRR.

THOSE *CHARACTERS*: THAT *DAME*, THE *SILK SPECTRE*; WHERE'S *SHE* NOW, I WONDER?

Panel 7:
...AND *RORSCHACH*, HEH! KNOW WHAT HE HAD IN HIS *POCKETS* WHEN WE *COLLARED* HIM?

SUGAR CUBES. WEIRD *SHIT*, HUH?

I'LL BE SEEING YOU, MR. DREIBERG. YOU TAKE *CARE*, NOW.

I WILL. GOOD EVENING, DETECTIVE.

Panel 8:
DAN? WHO WAS *THAT*? I WAS JUST IN THE *BATH* BUT I HEARD THE *LAST* OF IT.

WHAT HE SAID ABOUT 1977... WHAT DID IT *MEAN*?

Panel 9:
IT MEANS TIME'S RUNNING *OUT*. MAYBE HE'S ALREADY CALLED *ROCKEFELLER BASE*. MAYBE HE ALREADY KNOWS YOU'RE *HERE*. SPRINGING RORSCHACH ANY LATER THAN *TOMORROW* ISN'T *SAFE*.

SUDDENLY, WE HAVE A *DEADLINE*.

9

15

...EXTINGUISHED! ALL THE LIGHTS, THEY JUST WENT OUT...

SPEAK UP, I CAN HARDLY HEAR YOU.

IT'S SOME SORT OF POWER FAILURE, OBVIOUSLY. EMERGENCY LIGHTS SHOULD KICK IN SOON, PROVIDING NOBODY'S BEEN TOO ROUGH WITH THE ELECTRICALS.

DAN, THIS IS HORRIBLE. WHEN WE HEARD ABOUT THE RIOT, I THOUGHT IT WOULD JUST PROVIDE COVER FOR THE ESCAPE. I HADN'T IMAGINED THIS...

OLD GRUDGES GET WORKED OUT IN THESE THINGS.

OLD GRUDGES AND BAD BLOOD.

BUT THIS IS PANDEMONIUM! EVEN ASSUMING THAT NOBODY KILLED HIM ALREADY, THAT HE'S STILL ALIVE; HOW ARE WE SUPPOSED TO FIND HIM?

HE'S SUPPOSEDLY IN THE SOLITARY SECTION. HE SHOULDN'T BE TOO DIFFICULT TO TRACK DOWN...

I STILL DON'T SEE YOU NEED HIM. WHAT DID HE DO FOR YOU LATELY?

NOTHING. BUT MEETING HIM RECENTLY, IT'S LIKE HE WANTS TO MAKE FRIENDS WITHOUT KNOWING HOW.

AS IF THE GAP BETWEEN US WERE NARROWING.

IT'S JUST SO HARD, REACHING HIM. I MEAN, ALL THIS STUFF, THIS HORROR AND MADNESS, HE ATTRACTS IT. IT'S HIS WORLD. THIS IS WHERE HE LIVES...

...IN THIS SORDID, VIOLENT TWILIGHT ZONE...

UNDER THIS SHADOW.

18

WELL? DID WE FIND THE RIGHT *CELL*? IS HE *THERE*?

FROM THE *SMELL*, THIS WHOLE *PLACE* HAS HIS *STAMP* ON IT.

NO. NO, HE ISN'T HERE...

...BUT I THINK HE'S *BEEN* HERE.

COME ON. IF WE DON'T FIND HIM *SOON*, OUR WHOLE *PLAN* IS IN THE *TOILET*.

ALONG *HERE*, MAYBE?

I DON'T KNOW. IF ONLY THERE WAS SOME *SIGN*...

HEY! IS *THAT* HIM ALONG *THERE*? THERE WAS THAT *PICTURE* IN THE PAPERS, HIM WITHOUT HIS *MASK*...

I--I'M NOT *SURE*. IT LOOKS LIKE HIS *POSTURE* ...

HEY, RORSCHACH?

RORSCHACH? IS THAT ...? YES. YES, IT'S YOU.

COME ON, MAN. WE CAME TO BUST YOU *OUT* AND WE BETTER *HURRY* BEFORE, UH....

UH, WE'RE NOT *INTERRUPTING* ANYTHING?

19

NO.

EXCUSE ME. HAVE TO VISIT MEN'S ROOM.

OH, FOR CHRIST'S **SAKE**...

UH, LOOK, IT'S **OKAY**. I MEAN, IT HAPPENS TO **EVERYBODY**, RIGHT?

I REMEMBER ONCE I LOST A BIG **ARREST** LIKE THAT...

I WAS CLOSING ON THIS **DOPE DEALER** AND I NEEDED TO TAKE A LEAK. BY THE TIME I'D GOT IN AND OUT OF MY **COSTUME**, HE'D **VANISHED**.

I RE-DESIGNED IT SINCE THEN.

OH, SURE. EVERYBODY'S DONE THAT...

WHAT **PISSES ME** OFF, WE CAME TO **RESCUE** HIM, HE DOESN'T EVEN **THANK US!** DOESN'T EVEN SAY **HELLO!**

HELL, WHAT'S HE **DOING** IN THERE? THAT **BUMPING**...

IT'S **OKAY**... I THINK I JUST HEARD HIM **FLUSH**...

AT LAST!

SHHH.

THERE. DID WHAT HAD TO BE DONE. CAN LEAVE NOW.

REALLY? I MEAN, ARE YOU **SURE**? WE DON'T WANT TO GET TOO **RECKLESS** AND GO DIVING HEAD-FIRST **INTO** THINGS!

HURM.

GOOD ADVICE.

SURE THERE ARE MANY WHO'D AGREE WITH YOU.

20

INCIDENTALLY, GOOD SEEING YOU IN UNIFORM, DANIEL. LIKE OLD TIMES.

AND MISS JUSPECZYK. ALTHOUGH NEVER LIKED YOUR UNIFORM. NOTHING PERSONAL.

UH, MAYBE I BETTER KILL THE *SCREECHERS* SO ARCHIE DOESN'T *DEAFEN* YOU WHEN I BRING HIM *UP.*

HURRM. OWLSHIP. SCREECHERS. BELT CONSOLE. ALL THE OLD TOYS. I REMEMBER.

WHAT BROUGHT YOU OUT OF RETIREMENT? TAKING MASK KILLER SERIOUSLY AT LAST?

WELL...

NO. LEASTWAYS, *I'M* NOT.

NO? BUT THEN YOU HAVEN'T BEEN ATTACKED YET. FUNNY. MOST EVERYONE ELSE HAS.

RORSCHACH, FOR GOD'S *SAKE,* MAN, DON'T YOU *EVER* LET UP? SHE JUST *RESCUED* YOU...

WHAT'S HE *IMPLYING*? I JUST DON'T BUY THIS *CONSPIRACY* IS ALL!

I MEAN, TO ME, THIS WHOLE *SITUATION'S* GROTESQUE. DAN THOUGHT SPRINGING YOU MIGHT HELP; I PLAYED ALONG.

FRANKLY, I WISH I *HADN'T.* I WISH *JON* WAS HERE TO *STRAIGHTEN* EVERYTHING AND...

OH, *DAN,* I'M *SORRY.*

FORGET IT. HERE'S *ARCHIE...*

HURRY. WITHOUT THE *SCREECHERS* KEEPING FOLK *AWAY* WE'LL SOON START DRAWING *FIRE.*

ALSO, I WANT TO VISIT MY PLACE ONE LAST TIME BEFORE *THIS* CAPER BRINGS THE *POLICE* DOWN ON IT. THERE'S *EQUIPMENT* TO COLLECT.

Y'KNOW, THIS IS GETTING *HEAVY.* AS DAN *DREIBERG,* YOU'LL BE *WANTED.*

THE WORLD SHOULD *LAST* SO LONG. NO, IT'S OKAY. I SET UP *EMERGENCY* IDENTITIES *YEARS* AGO. *THEY'LL* CONCEAL US.

HOLD *TIGHT.* WE'RE GOING HOME TO *ROOST...*

27

HHUUGGHH

DERF? DERF, WHAT DID YOU DO? THESE KATIES I CAN'T '''

SHUT UP. WE'RE FINISHED HERE.

BUT DERF, I MEAN, SHIT, MAN, LOOK AT THE GUY! YOU...

I SAID WE'RE FINISHED HERE. LET'S GO.

MR. MASON? IT'S US, SAME AS LAST YEAR. WERE THOSE GUYS WHO JUST LEFT FRIENDS OF YOURS?

MR. MASON? HEY, C'MON. TRICK OR TREAT?

MR. MASON?

On Hallowe'en the old ghosts come about us, and they speak to some; to others they are dumb.

—*Hallowe'en*
Eleanor Farjeon

28

BANNER →

Thursday, October 31st, 1985

50 cents

NEW FRONTIERSMAN

Issue IVII
No. 21

★★★★ ▬▬▬▬▬▬▬▬▬▬

HONOR IS LIKE THE HAWK: SOMETIMES IT MUST GO HOODED

Hector Godfrey, *Editor*

RED ARMAGEDDON!

In this, the eleventh hour, with the world poised on the brink of Red Armageddon, it is vital that we, as a nation, should rally around those symbols that are closest to the great, warm, red-white-and-blue beating heart of this beleaguered country. They are our hope and our inspiration, the legends that urge our people onward even in times of deepest crisis.

Would our sense of national identity, our pride, our sense of honor; would these things be so enduring were it not for such great symbols of freedom as Paul Revere's midnight ride, or the Alamo, or the Gettysburg address? I think not. And yet, it seems there are those who, even in the dire adversity that besets us, see fit to ridicule and deride the very notions that have made America what she is today!

← cont. on pg. 2

Honor is like . . . (cont.)

WHO THE HELL DO THEY THINK THEY ARE?

For any citizen who has been watching the newsstands over this last, unbearable month, there can be little doubt who I am referring to. In the current edition of pseudo-intellectual Marxist-brat rock-star monthly *Nova Express*, cocaine-advocating editor DOUGLAS ROTH makes a vitriolic and unfounded attack upon the tradition of the masked lawman in our culture and attempts to stir up old prejudices and hatreds into a bloody wave of civil disorder.

It is hardly necessary for me to remind readers that in a previous edition of his inflammatory publication, Roth had spearheaded the cancer-smear character assassination of Dr. Manhattan. This wild and hysterical attack led to our country's greatest tactical asset leaving this world for self-imposed exile upon another. Ultimately, it may lead to searing nuclear apocalypse or our subjugation as a nation beneath the cossack boot of the U.S.S.R.

Nova Express, heaping libel upon libel, has followed up this potentially catastrophic feature with an article in its current edition that attempts to draw tenuous links between recent news items involving former masked adventurers and work them into some wild-eyed conspiracy theory, apparently forgetting that most of the "news items" involved were generated as a direct result of *Nova Express* and its irresponsible scaremongering! Roth refers gloatingly in his article to the fact that back copies of the *New Frontiersman* were found in the rented apartment of captured vigilante Rorschach after his arrest, citing this as "proof" of the aforementioned hero's poor character. He seems to suggest, with typical pothead disregard for logic, that Rorschach must be bad if he reads the *New Frontiersman*, while simultaneously implying that the *New Frontiersman* must be slightly disreputable if someone like Rorschach reads it! The overall effect of the piece is that of a snotty-nosed and unsubstantiated attack not only upon this paper and upon the individual costumed adventurers themselves, but also upon a whole American institution! Who the hell do Roth and his cringing staff of pinko sycophants think they are???

RIPPED OUT GUTS

The institution that Roth and his cronies are so casually ripping the guts out of is that of hooded justice, of a force for righteousness that dares to tread where the wimpy and useless laws laid down by the spineless dupes and fellow travellers in our judiciary forbid it to.

What about the Boston Tea Party? What about the spirit of the Lone Ranger? What about all those occasions when men have found it necessary to go masked in order to preserve justice above the letter of the law? *Nova Express* makes many sneering references to costumed heroes as direct descendants of the Ku Klux Klan, but might I point out that despite what some might view as their later excesses, the Klan originally came into being because decent people had perfectly reasonable fears for the safety of their persons and belongings when forced into proximity with people from a culture far less morally advanced.

No, the Klan were not strictly legal, but they did work voluntarily to preserve American culture in areas where there were very real dangers of that culture being overrun and mongrelized. Similarly, during our perfectly justified retaliatory bombing of Beirut in 1979, there were many of our so-called fair-weather-friend European allies who were bleating about supposed infringements of international law. Yet what are laws made for, if not to serve mankind? And if those laws through unforeseen circumstance become no longer applicable, is it not more noble to follow the course of right and justice; to serve the spirit of the law rather than its every dot and comma? In my book, anyone answering that question in the negative is someone without the moral backbone necessary to call himself an American. In the case of the *Nova Express* articles and their perpetrators, I would go so far as to call such a denial of time-tested patriotic virtues as being most definitely ANTI-American.

COKED-OUT COMMIE COWARDS

I've had it up to here with those coked-out commie cowards, and I think it's time we started to ask ourselves just who stands to benefit most from *Nova Express'* ridiculing of American legends and the subsequent subversion and undermining of our national morale? Can there be any doubt that the only beneficiary is the cause of international communism? Should we not perhaps call upon our authorities to take a closer look at exactly who is funding this pernicious piece of propaganda in pop star's

cont. on pg. 3

(open up
para. #

As we see it . . .

Honor is like . . . (cont.)

clothing that finds its way onto our newsstands each week? Regular readers will know that I have already voiced my suspicions concerning a red hand in the denunciation and subsequent exile of Dr. Manhattan (see *N.F.*, Sunday 20th October: "Our country's protector smeared by the Kremlin") and will no doubt join me in perceiving this renewed assault by *Nova Express* upon our traditions and values as further proof of where that magazine's interests lie: Due East, and don't you forget it.

Hector Godfrey, Editor

Photo to come

MISSING WRITER
VANISHED PERSONS LIST
GROWS AS HUNT CALLED OFF

Earlier this week, police called off their inquiry into the mysterious disappearance of author Max Shea, citing lack of evidence as a principal contributing factor in their decision. *New Frontiersman* would like to remind both the authorities concerned and our readers of the overwhelming evidence already tabulated by this paper to suggest that Shea's disappearance was part of a carefully orchestrated conspiracy, the roots of which may yet be traced back to sinister Cuban interests.

Although it is true to say that Shea did indeed vanish without trace, leaving no clue whatsoever as to his destination, by considering the extraordinary amount of similar disappearances reported at approximately the same time, it is possible to glimpse a larger and more frightening picture as it emerges. In the two months leading up to Shea's disappearance, no less than four prominent creative figures also seemingly dropped from the face of the earth. These included radical architect Norman Leith, surrealist painter Hira Manish, and respected "hard" science fiction author James Trafford March. Admittedly, the circumstances in each case are wildly different and seem to allow for a simple, meaningless coincidence of human destinies . . . Manish was apparently suffering profound difficulties with her marriage, making her apparent abandonment of her husband and two sons somewhat less than surprising. March owed massive debts to the IRS, who had frozen his earnings. Leith was reportedly depressed and even suicidal during the run-up to his disappearance, as was fellow missing person, avant-garde composer Linette Paley. As reasons for disappearance, these each seem individually credible enough to make any notion of conspiracy unnecessary, and yet a doubt still remains: Can *four* such prominent people simply dematerialize in the space of half as many months, leaving such bright and promising careers and reputations behind them?

Added to this, we must consider those prominent people in other fields, who, although less prominent and thus less easy to gauge numerically, have also apparently melted into thin air during this period. I have on record an unusually high number of disappearances from amongst the scientific community, which, although consisting largely of semi-skilled menial workers, does include such notable names as that of Dr. Whittaker Furnesse, the brilliant eugenics specialist who according to his wife left the family home one evening to walk the family dog and quite simply never returned.

Odder still, and quite probably entirely unconnected, there is the disappearance of *part* of a person after his death, recorded on the same week Shea's vanishing act reached the public awareness. Parents and relatives of so-called psychic and clairvoyant Robert Deschaines, attending his funeral following the young medium's fatal stroke, were horrified to learn that ghoulish vandals or practical jokers had stolen the corpse's head from its body while it lay unattended upon a mortuary slab. Police voiced a few tenuous opinions concerning possible involvement by black magic cultists, but since then no further evidence has come to light.

Even discounting this last curiosity, is there nobody who is prepared to look into this bizarre glut of disappearances and see what emerges? Can it be that our increasingly shrill and nervous judiciary are actually afraid to look too far under this particular rug for fear of what they might find hidden there? The *New Frontiersman* repeats it warning: Talented and prominent Americans are being spirited away from under our noses.

Isn't it time somebody found out just where they are going?

Photo to Come

THE DARKNESS OF MERE BEING

LAURIE? WHAT'S ...?

OH.

OF COURSE.

PLEASE FORGIVE ME...

SOMETIMES THESE THINGS SLIP MY MIND.

‹HHHUUHHHHR›

...SHOUTED AT HIM, HE LOOKED *SURPRISED*, COULDN'T IMAGINE WHY I'D BEAR A GRUDGE. SEE, IT'S *DIFFERENT* FOR HIM, AND I JUST COULDN'T *SUSTAIN* IT, THE *ANGER*...

GOD, YOU KNOW, REALLY, YOU NEED ANALYSIS, I'M SERIOUS...

HOW WOULD *YOU* KNOW HOW A WOMAN FEELS? SHIT, HOW A *MAN* FEELS, FOR THAT MATTER?

OH, THAT'S *CHEAP*. EVEN FOR *YOU*, THAT IS *CHEAP*!

WELL, C'MON, LET'S HEAR THE *REST*...

WHY? SO YOU CAN PUT IT IN A LETTER TO ONE OF THOSE *MAGAZINES* YOU READ? "MY WIFE DESCRIBED HOW HIS ROUGH HANDS SLOWLY SQUEEZED..."

STOP THAT!

YOU WANTED TO *HEAR*, SO *OKAY*, YOU *LISTEN*:

FIRST OFF, HE WAS *THERE*, RIGHT?

PLUS, HE WAS *GENTLE*. YOU KNOW WHAT GENTLENESS *MEANS* IN A GUY LIKE THAT? EVEN A *GLIMMER* OF IT?

OH *SPARE* ME.

IT MEANS YOU *REACHED* SOMETHING. IT MEANS YOU REACHED SOME OF THAT MAGICAL ROMANCE AND BULLSHIT THAT THEY PROMISE YOU WHEN YOU'RE A *KID*...

IT *ALSO* MEANS A BROKEN *MARRIAGE*; AN UNCERTAIN *FUTURE* FOR OUR *CHILD*...

MY CHILD. THAT'S WHAT ALL THIS IS *ABOUT*, REMEMBER?

ANY WAY, DON'T YOU WORRY ABOUT *HER* FUTURE. THAT'S TAKEN *CARE* OF.

"I TIPTOED DOWNSTAIRS TO THE T.V. ROOM. IT WAS DARK AND NEXT DOOR THEY WERE SHOUTING...

"NOBODY KNEW I WAS THERE. THESE MOMENTS WERE JUST MINE. EVERYTHING FELT *SECRET* AND *ENCHANTED*...

"...AND THERE WAS THIS *TOY*, THIS SNOWSTORM BALL, WITH A TINY *CASTLE* INSIDE, EXCEPT IT WAS LIKE A WHOLE *WORLD*; A WORLD INSIDE THE *BALL*...

"IT WAS LIKE A LITTLE GLASS BUBBLE OF SOMEWHERE *ELSE*.

"I LIFTED IT, STARTING A *BLIZZARD*. I KNEW IT WASN'T *REAL* SNOW, BUT I COULDN'T UNDERSTAND HOW IT FELL SO *SLOWLY*.

"I FIGURED INSIDE THE BALL WAS SOME DIFFERENT SORT OF *TIME*.

"*SLOW TIME*."

7

"AND THEN..."

LAUREL JANE?

AAA!

WHAT ARE YOU DOING DOWN HERE? WHAT...

LARRY, DON'T YOU *DARE* TAKE THIS OUT ON HER! SHE'S ONLY A *KID!* SHE'S VULNERABLE...

"...FRAGILE..."

"...AND INSIDE THERE WAS ONLY WATER.

"MY DAD YELLED AND SENT ME TO BED. HE WAS ALWAYS YELLING, PROBABLY BECAUSE HE KNEW I WASN'T *HIS*.

"MY REAL DAD, I'M PRETTY SURE, WAS MOM'S OLD BOYFRIEND, HOODED JUSTICE."

I SEE. THEN YOUR MOTHER'S HUSBAND WASN'T ...AHH. LOOK OVER THERE: A DUST STORM RISING.

YEAH. VERY NICE.

NO, SCHEXNAYDER WASN'T ANYTHING EXCEPT A DOMINEERING *BULLY*. HE REALLY USED TO *PICK* ON ME.

THAT'S PROBABLY WHY I'M *EDGY* IN RELATIONSHIPS WITH STRONG, *FORCEFUL* GUYS...

I MEAN, WITH *DAN*, IT ISN'T *LIKE* THAT. AS A *LOVER* HE'S MORE SORT OF *RECEPTIVE*; THE TYPE YOU CAN POUR YOUR *TROUBLES* OUT TO...

YOU MEAN THAT YOU'RE SLEEPING WITH DREIBERG?

B--BUT ...YOU ALREADY *KNOW*. I MEAN, YOU SAID...

I *SAID*, OFTEN, THAT YOU WERE MY ONLY *LINK*, MY ONLY CONCERN WITH THE WORLD.

WHEN YOU LEFT ME, I LEFT EARTH. DOES *THAT* NOT SAY SOMETHING?

NOW YOU HAVE REPLACED ME, AND THAT LINK IS SHATTERED. DON'T YOU SEE WHAT THAT MEANS?

DON'T YOU SEE THE FUTILITY OF ASKING ME TO SAVE A WORLD THAT I NO LONGER HAVE ANY STAKE IN?

8

≥HAAHHH≥

...AGREE. IT'S FUN SEEING ALL YOU GUYS AND... ONCE IN A WHILE, BUT... POINT, REALLY? I MEAN ...THOSE YEARS WE WORKED OUR ASSES ...DID WE ACHIEVE?

SHOULDN'T HAVE TO ASK, HOL. WE'RE AN INSPIRATION... THAT NEW BOY ...PAPERS...FEEL PROUD?

...ELL, AS FOR ME... WHAT I ACHIEVED... SITTING ...ON IT ...AND AS WHAT I ACHIEVED IT WITH ...

...I'M SITTING ON IT! HA HA HA HA HA!

AHEH. SALLY, REALLY ...

UH-OH. BETTER CLEAN UP YOUR ACT, SAL. WE GOT COMPANY.

AAH, SHE'S HEARD IT ALL BEFORE.

HI THERE, SUGAR TUSH. HOW'D THE WORKOUT GO? YOU GONNA BE A BIG TOUGH SUPER-LADY, LIKE MOM?

YEAH. I GUESS.

ATTA GIRL. NOW LEMME SEE... UNCLE HOLLIS YOU KNOW, BUT THIS BIG HUNK OVER HERE, THIS IS YOUR UNCLE NELSON. YOU'VE SEEN THE PICTURE...

OH, YEAH. CAPTAIN METROPOLIS. YOU WERE SKINNIER BACK THEN.

UH... RIGHT.

UH, WELL, LISTEN, SALLY, I'D BETTER GO CHECK OUTSIDE. HE SHOULD ARRIVE SOON, AND I PROMISED I'D MEET HIM...

HI THERE, PUMPKIN. SO, DID YOU READ MY BOOK YET?

SURE.

BOOK?

SURE. "UNDER THE HOOD." I GAVE SALLY ONE TO PASS ON...

I, UH, I DIDN'T GIVE IT TO HER YET. I FIGURED "SHE'S YOUNG, SHE DON'T WANNA READ THAT OLD STUFF."

MAYBE WHEN YOU'RE OLDER...

11

"I REMEMBER STARING AT *YOU*. I JUST COULDN'T GET USED TO YOU. I MEAN, YOU HAD A GREAT BODY, BUT, Y'KNOW, IT WAS *BLUE*.

"YOUR *GIRLFRIEND*, JANEY, SHE GLARED AT ME ALL THE WAY THROUGH.

"THEN IT *COLLAPSED*: EVERYBODY *LEAVING* EXCEPT NELSON AND ADRIAN. BIG DISAPPOINTMENT...

"I GUESS I SORTA WONDERED WHAT IT WOULD BE LIKE, SLEEPING WITH YOU, BUT YOU SEEMED KINDA SPOKEN FOR. NOBODY ELSE THERE INTERESTED ME.

"OUTSIDE, I WATCHED THEM GO: DAN IN HIS SHIP, RORSCHACH SNEAKING AWAY INTO THE BUSHES. HE GAVE ME THE CREEPS.

"I FELT LET DOWN, RESTLESS, HORNY AND I NEEDED A CIGARETTE. I WAS LEAVING NELSON'S MANSION...

"...WHEN SOMEBODY CALLED MY NAME."

LAUREL? LAUREL JANE, IS THAT RIGHT?

SO YOU'RE SALLY'S KID?

UH, YEAH. YEAH. YOU'RE THE *COMEDIAN*. I CAUGHT YOUR ACT IN THERE. YOU WERE PRETTY COOL.

WELL YOU DON'T LOOK LIKE YOU GREW UP TOO BAD *YOURSELF*. HERE...LEMME TAKE A *LOOK*...

HEH. YEAH, THERE'S HER EYES...EVEN GOT THAT FUNNY LITTLE MOLE...

YOU AIN'T GOT HER HAIR, BUT OTHERWISE, YOU'RE LIKE HER. YOU'RE A LOOKER

WELL, UH, THANK YOU.

UH, SAY, I NEED A *CIGARETTE*, BUT I DON'T HAVE A *LIGHT*. DO YOU...?

SURE. HEY, LISTEN, YOUR *MOM*: SHE TALK ABOUT ME MUCH?

NO. NOT MUCH.

HEH. IT FIGURES. HERE'S YOUR LIGHT. I...

HELL. GONE OUT. HERE, LEMME...

IT'S OKAY. I'LL STEADY IT.

THERE. THAT'S BETTER.

YOU TAKE YOUR HANDS *OFF* HER!

15

IT STRETCHES MORE THAN THREE THOUSAND MILES, SO THAT ONE END KNOWS DAY WHILE THE OTHER ENDURES NIGHT.

TEMPERATURE DIFFERENCES BREED SHRIEKING WINDS THAT HERD OCEANS OF FOG ALONG A CANYON FOUR MILES DEEP.

DOES THE HUMAN HEART KNOW CHASMS SO ABYSMAL?

YES! YES, MINE, RIGHT NOW! JON, YOU'VE SEEN PEOPLE DEPRESSED. ME, WHEN I'M MISERABLE, WHEN I'VE HAD TOO MUCH TO DRINK...

YES. I REMEMBER A BANQUET IN 1973...

OH, DON'T REMIND ME. I ACTED LIKE AN IDIOT...

...BUT I GUESS THAT'S IN KEEPING WITH THE REST OF MY LIFE, HUH? I MEAN, YOU SAY IT'S ALL WORTHLESS, RIGHT? THAT WE'RE ALL BLIND, STUPID THINGS, STUMBLING THROUGH OUR LIVES...

"...HOPELESSLY LOST IN THE FOG."

19

BEFORE YOU *HIT* HER? BEFORE YOU *KICKED* HER? THAT ISN'T THE WAY YOU TREAT *PEACHES?*

UH, MISS JUSPECZYK...

SOMEBODY GET HER *BOYFRIEND.*

KID, ARE YOU SURE YOU WANNA TAKE THIS ALL THE WAY?

DAMN *STRAIGHT;* DAMN *STRAIGHT* I DO! I MEAN, WHAT KIND OF MAN *ARE* YOU, YOU HAVE TO TAKE SOME WOMAN, YOU HAVE TO FORCE HER INTO HAVING SEX AGAINST HER *WILL...*

ONLY ONCE.

"ONLY *ONCE,* AS IF, Y'KNOW, IT WAS BETTER THAN DOING IT TWICE OR FIFTY TIMES! AND HIS *SCAR...* IT ALWAYS LOOKED LIKE HE WAS *SNEERING...*

"HAD SEVEN SCOTCHES INSIDE ME, ONE IN MY HAND...

"I LET HIM HAVE IT."

...AND THEN YOU CAME, AND YOU WERE ANGRY, AND YOU TOOK ME HOME.

IT WAS THE FIRST TIME YOU EVER TELEPORTED ME ANYWHERE...

FIRST TIME I THREW UP.

...BUT, I MEAN, WHY BOTHER TELLING YOU ALL THIS? IT JUST *CONFIRMS* THINGS, RIGHT? ALL THESE WRETCHED, GRUBBY LITTLE HUMAN ENCOUNTERS: BETTER OFF WITHOUT 'EM!

NONE OF IT EVER MEANT A *DAMN* THING, ANYWAY.

I MEAN, THESE, MY MOTHER'S *CLIPPINGS;* HER WHOLE *LIFE,* RIGHT *THERE!* WHAT'S IT *MEAN?*

IN *YOUR* TERMS, NEXT TO A...A *NEUTRINO,* NEXT TO SOMETHING YOU CAN'T EVEN *SEE,* FOR CHRIST'S SAKE? IT MEANS *NOTHING!*

LAURIE...

DON'T *"LAURIE"* ME! IT'S POINTLESS *DEBATING* WHEN YOU OBVIOUSLY DON'T SEE ANYTHING TERRIBLY *MIRACULOUS* IN LIFE. MAYBE QUANTUM PHYSICS DOESN'T *ALLOW* MIRACLES...

NO. "THERMODYNAMIC MIRACLES" ARE...

OH, FOR GOD'S *SAKE,* JON, JUST *LAND* THIS THING.

NOW.

21

23

25

26

"COME... DRY YOUR EYES, FOR YOU ARE *LIFE*, RARER THAN A *QUARK* AND UNPREDICTABLE BEYOND THE DREAMS OF *HEISENBERG*; THE CLAY IN WHICH THE FORCES THAT SHAPE ALL THINGS LEAVE THEIR FINGERPRINTS MOST *CLEARLY*.

" DRY YOUR EYES...

"...AND LET'S GO HOME."

As far as we can discern, the sole purpose of human existence is to kindle a light of meaning in the darkness of mere being.

—C. G. Jung
MEMORIES, DREAMS, REFLECTIONS

DAILY WORLD

January 12, 1939   *More than news!*   5 c

VILLAINS VIE FOR VOLUPTUOUS VIGILANTE

Goons are going ga-ga over the latest do-gooder to pull on a tight costume and jump aboard the masked vigilante bandwagon. Why? Well, maybe it's because *this* costumed cutie is a *girl!* Shapely 18-year-old redhead Sally Jupiter (36-24-36) has taken the alluring and mysterious monicker of "Silk Spectre" as she dons the shortest long underwear yet and becomes the first feisty female to join the fight against felony.

Miss Jupiter's agent, Mr. Larry Schexnayder, says that former waitress and burlesque dancer Sally is such a hit with the hoods that they're practically tripping over each other in the rush to get nabbed by her! In testimony, he produced Mr. Claude Boke of no fixed address, currently out on parole after Sally, who happened to be on hand, arrested him during an attempted liquor store robbery.

"She beat me fair and square, but I don't hold no grudges. She's a pretty-looking young woman and I'd rather have her take me in than two fat old cops anytime," says Claude, who received a light fine and has since quit drinking and taken a job pumping gasoline.

Sally, who eventually hopes to move on to modeling work or movies, tells us that there is already a movie about her life in the works.

"It's called 'Silk Spectre: The Sally Jupiter Story,'" enthuses Sally, "and it's already in the planning stages. Larry and I have met with Mr. King Taylor of Hollywood, and everybody's very excited about it all."

I'm sure we all wish spunky Sal luck in her future endeavors, and if the above movie gets made, who knows? Maybe Sally will have to organize a special premiere . . . just for the criminal fraternity!

reports are true, she certainly has some explaining to do to her hubby and two kids back home on the ranch.

• • •

Meanwhile, over with the cape-and-mask crowd, lips are buzzing and tongues are wagging about cheesecake crime-crusher **Sally Jupiter**, alias the **SILK SPECTRE.** It seems that she and veteran vigilante **HOODED JUSTICE** are something of an item, and seldom out of each other's company. Can wedding bells be too far away? If you want evidence, just look whose arm our Sal is hanging onto in the recently released publicity photographs of that tights-and-trunk-clad team, **The Minutemen.** Between you and me, your Zelda wonders: Does he keep that hood and noose on *all* the time?

• • •

Spotted dancing cheek to cheek at a certain

King Taylor Productions

8-22-45

Sal and Larry,

Hi, kids! I know, I know, it's been ages, but I think things are finally moving with "She Devils In Silk." (That's the latest title, by the way. Maurie dreamed it up. Hope you like it. We decided that "Sally Jupiter: Law In Its Lingerie" was too long, after all.)

The latest version is looking good—we've retained a lot of the plot elements from the saturday morning Matinee approach we adopted after junking the documentary idea, and we've kept a lot of the footage we shot with you way back then. This new version has some added material to make it accessible to a more adult market, and I think you'll find it kinda fun. We have a young discovery named Cherry Dean that I'm very excited about, and she stands in for you in the new scenes. From the back, she's a dead ringer! It's phenomenal!

Anyway, I'll keep touching base with you as things progress.

Hugs and kisses,

King

Dear Miss Jupiter,

Having seen you in the news lately, I wished to introduce myself. My name is Captain Metropolis, and I too am a costumed adventurer,
with a keen interest in stamping out crime and injustice wheresoever
it should rear its ugly head. I am delighted to find that you share
these inclinations.

I note also from my perusal of the press that there are several
other people of our persuasion stepping forward to join the struggle
across America, and, being a military man by nature and career it
struck me that it might be a distinct strategic advantage if we were
to organize ourselves into some sort of battalion, ready to do our
country's bidding at a moment's notice.

I suggest that such a group might be called 'The New Minute Men
of America', and I have already devised such things as codes and pass-
words and strategic exercises that would serve us well in our war on
infamy.

If you are interested in this proposal, please contact me through
my representative, former Marine Lieutenant Nelson Gardner, whose card
is enclosed.

I look forward very much to hearing from you.

Your costumed Comrade in the campaign against crime,

Captain Metropolis

Sally — thought there might be mileage in this — P.Rwise J.S.

Larry —
Jesus Christ! Are
you kidding—!

February 3rd, 1948

Dear Sally,

        Haven't been in touch lately because I thought you should have time to get over poor Bill's funeral. However, there's things that need talking over.

        Nelly called last night, upset over yet another tiff with H.J. Those two are getting worse. The more they row and act like an old married couple in public, the harder they are to cover for. I know that you've provided a pretty steady alibi for H.J. up to now, and that the publicity we got from that hasn't exactly hurt you either, but it can't last much longer. Nelly says he's always out when Nelly calls, out with boys, and apparently there's a lot of rough stuff going on. One of these punks only has to go to the cops with a convincing story and some convincing bruises to back it up and it would be the Silhouette fiasco all over again.

        I honestly wonder how long it can last. Lewis is drinking harder all the time, and has been very low since the thing with Bill. Mason is a big bouncy boy scout, same as ever, but with Nelly and H.J. acting up it's a pretty sorry spectacle at the meetings these days. Maybe now is the time to pull out and cut our losses. We've made quite a sum, you know, and I've often talked about a place out west somewhere; maybe now's the time we could take it on as a viable partnership proposition together? Anyways, at least think it over.

                        With fond regards,

Larry

nearest thing I ever got to a proposal

SCREEN REVIEWS

SILK SWINGERS OF SUBURBIA

DIR: Edmund "King" Taylor
STARRING: Cherry Dean, Rod Donovan, Dana Young, Lola Booker, Harry J. Peters, Sally Juniper.

If you like tasteful and sensually artistic modern cinema, then I recommend that this film be avoided at all costs. Cheaply made even by "B"-movie standards, this appears to have started life as a children's adventure serial, complete with unconvincing and dated footage of a stuntwoman in an antique chorus girl costume engaging in poorly staged fights with stock heavies. Edited into this unpromising and juvenile scenario with astonishing clumsiness, we have scenes of Miss Dean—similarly attired and being tied up, whipped and fondled by "Rod Donovan," who must surely be a relative of well-known hack director "King" Taylor, so close is the resemblance between the two men. Too awful even to be dignified with the term "pornography," the only real act of sadism in this film lies in releasing it; the only masochism in watching it.

PROBE PROFILE: SALLY JUPITER

an interview with a forties glamour girl and the seamier side of her crimefighting career.

PROBE: Sally, how much would you say that it's a sex thing, putting on a costume?

SALLY: No. I don't . . . Well, let me say this, for me, it was never a sex thing. It was a money thing. And I think for some people it was a fame thing, and for a tiny few, God bless 'em, I think it was a goodness thing. I mean, I'm not saying it wasn't a sex thing for some people, but, no, no, I wouldn't say that's what motivated the majority . . .

PROBE: There was Ursula Zandt, the Silhouette . . .

SALLY: Uh-huh. Well, sooner or later, okay, that's going to come up, so let me deal with that . . . First off, I didn't like her as a person. I mean, she was not an easy person to get along with. But, when the papers got hold of it, her being a—what is it—a gay woman they say nowadays, when that happened, I thought it was wrong. I mean, Laurence, who was my first husband, he got everybody to throw her out of the group to minimize the P.R. damage, but . . . I mean, I voted along with everybody else, but . . . well, it wasn't fair. It wasn't honest. I mean, she wasn't the only gay person in the Minutemen. Some professions, I don't know, they attract a certain type . . .

PROBE: Who else was gay?

SALLY: I'm not naming anybody. It was a couple of the guys, and they're both dead now. One died recently. I'm not saying who

it was, I'm just saying that we all knew, and we knew she wasn't the only one, and we slung her out just the same. When she got murdered like that . . . I mean, I never really liked her. Ursula. Was that her real name? I didn't know that. I didn't like her, but . . . throwing her out. We shouldn't have done that. I feel bad about that.

PROBE: On the subject of the Minutemen, in Hollis Mason's autobiography . . .

SALLY: Uh-oh! Here it comes.

PROBE: . . . he alleges that you were sexually assaulted by the Comedian, who, as you know, is still active. You've never said too much about this incident yourself . . .

SALLY: Well, why break a lifetime's habit?

PROBE: You won't comment upon that?

SALLY: I . . . Look, I don't bear any grudges. That's all. I know I should, everybody tells me I should but . . . look, I don't have to justify this, okay? It's just that nothing's that simple, not even things that are simply awful. You know, rape is rape and there's no excuses for it, absolutely none, but for me, I felt . . . I felt like I'd contributed in some way. Is that misplaced guilt, whatever my analyst said? I really felt that, that I was somehow as much to blame for . . . for letting myself be his victim not in a physical sense, but . . . but,

it's like what if, y'know? What if, just for a moment, maybe I really did want . . . I mean, that doesn't excuse him, doesn't excuse either of us, but with all that doubt, what it is to come to terms with it, I can't stay angry when I'm so uncertain about my own feelings . . .

PROBE: You're retired now, and it seems your daughter has been groomed to follow in your footsteps. Having seen the lifestyle for yourself, how do you feel about that?

SALLY: Mm. That's tough. I guess, in a lot of ways, it was me who pushed Laurie, that's my daughter, pushed her into this line of work . . . I know that when she's upset about something she always blames me for shoving her into such a weird career, but underneath somewhere, I think she secretly kinda likes it. She likes to bitch about it, but what else would she have done? Been a housewife? Got a job in a bank? So she didn't have a normal life! What's so great about normal life? Normal life stinks! You can ask anybody! No, no, of course, I'm her mother, I get worried about her. But in the end, I think she'll see what it was I gave her. I think she'll start to see her life next to the lives of other kids and she'll start thinking in terms of what I saved her from instead of what I condemned her to.

PROBE: You think so?

SALLY: I hope so.

"You know, rape is rape and there's no excuse for it, absolutely none, but for me, I felt . . . I felt like I'd contributed in some way."

' "VO PIDEPS 'VEPE APPROACHING

THEY'RE IN THE 'COPTERS.

'COPTERS PROCEED TO ENTRANCE ALPHA. ENTRANCE ALPHA, STAND BY...

CARS ONE AND TWO NOW APPROACHING MAIN CONCOURSE...

THE PRESIDENTIAL PARTY IS NOW INSIDE THE COMPLEX. ENTRANCE ALPHA REMAIN OPEN UNTIL DEFCON ONE IS ACHIEVED. MAIN CONCOURSE, ALL UNITS PREPARE TO RECEIVE VISITORS ...

2

SO, ASSUMING YOUR SPARE OUTFIT'S WHERE YOU *LEFT* IT, WHERE DO WE START?

MAKE INQUIRIES AMONGST UNDERWORLD. WHATEVER'S BEHIND ELIMINATION OF MASKED HEROES IS SOMETHING BIG. MAKES RIPPLES. OUT THERE, SOMEWHERE... SOMEBODY KNOWS.

YEAH, I GUESS SO. ALSO, WITH THIS *MASK KILLER* THING, WE SHOULD CONTACT *ADRIAN*.

HURN. YES. PERHAPS HE'LL BE LESS DISMISSIVE OF IDEA AFTER ATTEMPT ON OWN LIFE... DOWN THIS WAY. REAR FIRE ESCAPE.

THE THING *IS*, WE'VE GOT SO LITTLE *TIME* TO FIGURE OUT WHO'S *DOING* THIS. I MEAN, NEUTRALIZING *JON*, FRAMING *YOU*, WE'RE TALKING SOMEBODY *MAJOR*.

YES. ALL ACCOMPLISHED SO EASILY. LESSON IN VULNERABILITY. MUST BE MORE CAREFUL IN FUTURE.

FUTURE? *WHAT* FUTURE?

MADISON SQUARE GARDEN

THAT'S MY WHOLE *POINT*: WE'RE LOOKING AT WORLD WAR THREE WITHIN THE *WEEK*!

I MEAN, WHAT DO WE *DO*? THE STAKES ARE SO *HIGH* AND HUMANITY IS SO CLOSE TO THE *EDGE*...

SOME OF US HAVE ALWAYS LIVED ON EDGE, DANIEL. IT IS POSSIBLE TO SURVIVE THERE IF YOU OBSERVE RULES!

JUST HANG ON BY FINGERNAILS... ...AND NEVER LOOK DOWN.

5

WELCOME BACK, SIR. IT IS GOOD TO HAVE YOU SAFE WITH US. WE RECEIVED BULLETINS FROM NEW YORK...

THE ATTEMPTED SHOOTING? AH YES. YES, THESE ARE DANGEROUS TIMES...

HELLO, BUBASTIS. HELLO, OLD GIRL.

DO YOU STILL WISH TO STUDY THE *MONITORS* AND RECORD YOUR *OB-SERVATIONS* BEFORE DINNER? IF YOU ARE *HUNGRY*...

NO. LET DINNER WAIT. THE WORK COMES FIRST, AS EVER. THERE ARE THINGS TO DO, PROBLEMS TO SOLVE...

IT'S THE SAME OLD STORY.

INCIDENTALLY, DID THE DELIVERY RUN SMOOTHLY IN MY ABSENCE?

OH YES. WE THREE SUPERVISED THE RECEPTION UN-AIDED, AS INSTRUCTED.

THE MONITORS HAVE BEEN PREPARED, SIR. HOW MANY SCREENS DID YOU WISH TO VIEW?

ALL OF THEM. RANDOM CHANNEL CHANGE EVERY HUNDRED SECONDS.

THE PLANET IS CURRENTLY SWARMING WITH EVENTS. IN SUCH TIMES, *NONE* OF THEM ARE INSIGNIFICANT.

I NEED INFORMATION. INFORMATION IN ITS MOST CONCENTRATED FORM.

HA HA! SIR, DO YOU NOT FEAR THAT YOU MIGHT BECOME *DRUNK* UPON SO CONCENTRATED A DRAFT OF KNOWLEDGE?

HA HA HA. NO, I DON'T THINK SO.

INDEED, IT IS THE MOST SOBERING POTION THAT I KNOW.

7

DON'T PLAY GAMES WITH ME. YOU WASTE TIME LOOKING FOR PATTERN WHEN PATTERN IS OBVIOUS. THE MASK KILLER...

IF YOU'D **LISTEN** THAT'S WHAT I'M TRYING TO **SAY!** WHAT IF THERE **IS** NO MASK KILLER?

LOOK, THE COMEDIAN LEARNED, **ACCIDENTALLY**, ABOUT SOME **ISLAND**, SOME SCHEME AGAINST **JON.** THE PLOT AGAINST JON COMES **FIRST.** BLAKE'S KILLED WHEN HE **DISCOVERS** IT.

WHO KNEW BLAKE SUSPECTED ANYTHING?

THIS **DIMENSIONAL DEVELOPMENTS** COMPANY EMPLOYED MOLOCH. MAYBE HIS PLACE WAS **BUGGED** WHEN BLAKE VISITED?

THAT'D ALSO EXPLAIN HOW THEY KNEW ABOUT **YOUR** INVESTIGATIONS AND WERE ABLE TO **FRAME** YOU...WITHOUT **REQUIRING** ANY 'MASK KILLER'.

AND VEIDT?

MM. ADRIAN'S A **PROBLEM.** THAT **WAS** A CLEAR-CUT ASSASSINATION ATTEMPT, USING A HIRED **KILLER**...

EXACTLY. SO TRACE KILLER. VISIT BARS. SQUEEZE PEOPLE. BEEN LAZING AROUND A LONG TIME. MAYBE YOU'VE FORGOTTEN HOW WE DO THINGS.

LAZING...?

LISTEN, I'VE **HAD** IT! WHO THE HELL DO YOU THINK YOU **ARE**? YOU **LIVE** OFF PEOPLE WHILE **INSULTING** THEM, NOBODY COMPLAINS BECAUSE THEY THINK YOU'RE A GODDAMNED **LUNATIC**...

YOU KNOW HOW **HARD** IT IS, BEING YOUR **FRIEND**?

I...LOOK, RORSCHACH, I'M **SORRY.** I SHOULDN'T HAVE SAID ALL THAT...

LISTEN, YOU'RE **RIGHT.** WE'VE BOTH BEEN DOWN HERE TOO LONG. IT MUST BE DARK ENOUGH TO SURFACE BY NOW. I'LL TAKE HIM UP.

DANIEL...

YOU ARE...A GOOD FRIEND. I KNOW THAT.

I AM SORRY...THAT IT IS SOMETIMES DIFFICULT.

UH...HEY...

HEY, FORGET IT. IT'S OKAY, MAN.

IT'S OKAY.

10

Y'KNOW, I DIDN'T EXPECT ALL THIS TO TAKE SO *LONG*. DIDN'T EXPECT THIS *WAITING*...

LOOK: EVERYBODY'S SCARED THEY'LL DROP IT TONIGHT, GATHERIN' ON CORNERS, LOOKING FOR *TROUBLE*...

AT DEATH'S APPROACH, ALL CREATURES DISCOVER AN APTITUDE FOR VIOLENCE.

THE VEIDT METHOD
I WILL GIVE YOU BODIES BEYOND YOUR WILDEST

FLAILING, SCRATCHING, SHE WAS A BRIAR ROSE IN THE WIND. THE WIND DROPPED. HER THRASHINGS BECAME WEAKER...

THE HORSES WATCHED, UNDERSTANDING ONLY A LITTLE.

LIKE, IT'S TOO BIG TO TAKE *IN*, BUT PEOPLE KNOW SOMETHING *BAD'S* HAPPENING...

Panel 3:

PEOPLE KNOW SOMETHING'S *COMING.*

ASK ME, IT'S *DOOMSDAY*, LIKE IN THE BOOK O' REVOLUTIONS. I MEAN, TANKS IN EAST GERMANY, THERE'S NO MISTAKIN' IT ...

WHEN DEATH WAS ASSURED, RESIGNATION LENT HER EYES A CERTAIN MATURITY.

THE VEIDT METHOD
I WILL GIVE YOU BODIES BEYOND YOUR WILDEST

Panel 4:

THUMBS CROSSED, I CLOSED HER WINDPIPE. A BUCCANEER'S WHORE DESERVED NO PITY.

EVENTUALLY I STOOD, LEGS TREMBLING, BARELY SUPPORTING ME. IN THE FOAM ABOUT MY ANKLES, TWO WORLDS LAY ENDED.

MAYBE TODAY, MAYBE TOMORROW, BUT *SOON* FOR *SURE.*

Panel 5:

GOOD DAY, SIR. I'D LIKE TO PURCHASE A GAZETTE, IF I MAY.

UH, SURE. THAT'S WHAT I'M *HERE* FOR...

MY PURPOSE ALMOST FORGOTTEN IN THE GIDDY WHIRL OF MURDER ITSELF, I GAZED STUPIDLY AT THE HORSES.

THE VEIDT METHOD
I WILL GIVE YOU BODIES BEYOND YOUR WILDEST

RECOVERING, I BECAME MORE RATIONAL. SEEKING VENGEANCE, MIGHT I TURN THIS UNFORESEEN CIRCUMSTANCE TO MY ADVANTAGE? AN IDEA BLOSSOMED, PLAUSIBLE, TEMPTING...

THERE. NOW, WE'VE BOUGHT ONE OF *YOUR* PAPERS. PERHAPS YOU'D LIKE TO TRY *OURS*?

Panel 7:

HUH?

I'LL EXPLAIN. YOU SEE, WE, LIKE MANY PEOPLE TODAY, BELIEVE GOD WILL SHORTLY END THE WORLD. HOW DOES THAT IDEA STRIKE YOU?

WATCH TOWER

THE NOTION FASCINATED ME. IT WAS TERRIBLE AND YET TERRIBLY CONVENIENT...

Panel 8:

BALONEY! END THE *WORLD*? NO WAY, JOSÉ!

OH. I SEE. WELL, WE'RE JUST *LEAVING* ...

THIS COUPLE LEFT DAVIDSTOWN UNHINDERED. DESPITE THE PIRATE SENTRIES THERE MUST BE THEY'D BE ALLOWED BACK, ALSO...

TIED TO HER SADDLE, SHE LOOKED QUITE NATURAL.

Panel 9:

GODDAMN *FANATICS.* ITCHIN' TO SAY " I *TOLD YA SO!* "

WOULDN'T GIVE 'EM THE *SATISFACTION* !

TWO FIGURES HAD RIDDEN HERE, NOW TWO RODE BACK. SOON. SOON I WOULD VENTURE AMONGST EVIL MEN, AND MAKE THEM FEAR ME...

UTOPIA
THE DAY THE EARTH STOOD STILL

New York Gazette

ASTERN EUROPE: TANKS MASS AS ONFLICT ESCALATES

13

FORGET IT, WHATEVER IT IS. I CAN'T WAIT UNTIL A HOTEL ON THE *MAINLAND*. AFTER YEARS WITH THAT *SEXLESS OAF* AND HIS SPOILED SONS, I'M *IMPATIENT*.

SOME KINDA *BOX* UNDER THE *TARPAULIN*. LEMME SWITCH THIS *LIGHT* ON ...

MAX, *PLEASE* ...

WHAT'S THAT *COUNTER*? LET ME *SEE* THAT. IT'S ...

MAX, FOR GOD'S SAKE, CONCENTRATE ON *ME*. THE CREW MUST *VISIT* THIS PART OF THE SHIP, AND I THINK WE MIGHT NOT HAVE VERY LONG.

MAX? YOU'RE SO *PALE*. WHAT'S *WRONG*?

NOTHING, LOVE.

NOTHING'S WRONG.

HOLD ME.

RORSCHACH'S JOURNAL. NOVEMBER 1ST, 1985.:

FINAL ENTRY? LEFT VEIDT'S OFFICE JUST BEFORE MIDNIGHT.

DREIBERG, CONVINCED VEIDT'S BEHIND EVERYTHING, IS SERIOUS ABOUT VISITING ANTARCTICA. OWLSHIP CAPABLE, APPARENTLY, BUT ARE WE?..

VEIDT. CANNOT IMAGINE MORE DANGEROUS OPPONENT.

ASSUMING JOURNEY POSSIBLE, TRACKING HIM TO HIS LAIR ONLY OPTION. STILL FEEL UNEASY. UNFAMILIAR TERRITORY...

HE COULD KILL US BOTH, THERE IN SNOW. NOBODY WOULD EVER KNOW...

FIRST NIGHT IN NOVEMBER.

I AM COLD TONIGHT.

VEIDT IS FASTER THAN DREIBERG. PERHAPS FASTER THAN ME. RETURN FROM MISSION SEEMS UNLIKELY.

THIS LAST ENTRY. WILL SHORTLY MAIL JOURNAL TO ONLY PEOPLE CAN TRUST.

TELL DREIBERG I NEED TO CHECK MY MAILDROP. HE BELIEVES ME.

APPRECIATE YOUR RECENT SUPPORT AND HOPE WORLD SURVIVES LONG ENOUGH FOR THIS TO REACH YOU, BUT TANKS ARE IN EAST BERLIN, AND WRITING IS ON WALL.

FOR MY OWN PART, REGRET NOTHING. HAVE LIVED LIFE, FREE FROM COMPROMISE...

OFFICES BELOW, HEADSTONES MARKING DAILY GRAVES OF THOUSANDS. INSIDE, ACROSS CLOCK FACES, AS OBSERVED AS THOSE OF CELEBRITIES, HANDS COMMENCE FINAL LAPS.

OBLIVION GALLOPS CLOSER, FAVORING THE SPUR, SPARING THE REIN.

I THINK WE WILL BE GONE SOON.

NOVEMBER 2ND
PALE HO[RSE]
IN CONCERT WITH
KRYSTALNAC[HT]
MADISON SQUARE

IF READING THIS NOW, WHETHER I AM ALIVE OR DEAD, YOU WILL KNOW TRUTH: WHATEVER PRECISE NATURE OF THIS CONSPIRACY, ADRIAN VEIDT RESPONSIBLE.

HAVE DONE BEST TO MAKE THIS LEGIBLE. BELIEVE IT PAINTS DISTURBING PICTURE.

...AND STEP INTO THE SHADOW NOW WITHOUT COMPLAINT.

RORSCHACH, NOVEMBER 1ST, 1985.

US MAIL
SAMEDAY MIDTOWN EXPRESS

22

US MAIL SORTING DEPOT

SNOW NOR
LOOM OF NIGHT
AY THESE COURI
HE SWIFT COMPLE
R APPOINTED TA

US MAIL

PIONEER PUBLISHING INC

MAIL FOR YA.

UH, THANKS...

SEYMOUR, BRING THAT IN HERE AND OPEN IT! MAYBE THAT LAZY JERK FEINBERG MANAGED TO GET HIS EDITORIAL CARTOON IN ON TIME!

NEW FRONTIERSMAN

I MEAN, RED HOLOCAUST ABOUT TO BREAK, EVERY-THING HAPPENING AT ONCE, AM I SUPPOSED TO HANDLE THINGS BY MYSELF?

UH, THIS FIRST ONE'S SOME JOURNAL...

"DEAD DOG IN ALLEY THIS MORNING, TIRE TREAD ON BURST STOMACH..."

JESUS, WHO'S IT FROM? SON OF SAM? SLING IT ON THE CRANK FILE. NEW YEAR, WE'LL BURN THAT GARBAGE HEAP AND START OVER!

HERE'S ONE ABOUT FLUORIDE TURNING PEOPLE INTO HOMOS...

CRANK FILE! THROW 'EM ALL ON THE CRANK FILE AND GET SOME WORK DONE!

WAR'S COMING, AND THIS PAPER HAS A MISSION, GODDAMNIT. I WON'T SEE TRUTH AND INTEGRITY BURIED BENEATH AN AVALANCHE OF DRIVEL!

WHILE WE STAND AROUND SORTING JUNK MAIL, WE COULD MISS SOMETHING IMPORTANT! HELL, FACE IT, THE REDS COULD HAVE EMPTIED THEIR SILOS FIVE MINUTES AGO...

THE BIRDS COULD BE IN THE AIR RIGHT NOW!

24

OW.

YOU OKAY?

TWISTED ANKLE. NOTHING SERIOUS. LANDED ON IT BADLY NIGHT POLICE TOOK ME.

HOW BAD IS DAMAGE TO SHIP?

DIFFICULT TO SAY. PROBABLY NOTHING I COULDN'T FIX GIVEN A FEW HOURS...

IT'D BE QUICKER TO COVER THE REMAINING DISTANCE ON THE HOVERBIKES. THE INSTRUMENTS PUT US WITHIN TWENTY MILES OF VEIDT'S FORTRESS.

YOU BREAK OUT THE BIKES WHILE I GET INTO MY SNOW SUIT.

UH... YOU'RE SURE I CAN'T FIT YOU OUT IN SOMETHING A LITTLE WARMER?

FINE LIKE THIS.

WELL, WHATEVER YOU WANT. GIVE ME A SECOND AND I'LL OPEN THE REAR DOOR SO YOU CAN UNLOAD THOSE...

USED THESE WHEN WE TOOK UNDERBOSS. REMEMBER RIDING ALONG SEWER.

GOD, YES! THEY KNEW WE COULDN'T GET ARCHIE DOWN THERE AND FIGURED THEY WERE SAFE...

THEN YOU SHOOT OUT OF THAT TUNNEL, WITH THE GAS CLOUD, ALL THE RATS RUNNING AHEAD OF YOU...

MAN, THEIR FACES!

YES. GOOD NIGHT. THINK OF IT OFTEN.

AS I RECALL, CONTROLS SIMPLE; JUST TWO PEDALS AND STEERING COLUMN.

YOU GOT IT.

TCH. LOOK AT THAT ICE. BETTER FIX IT SOON AS WE GET BACK...

IF WE GET BACK.

YEAH.

YEAH. IF WE GET BACK. I'M GOING TO SECURE THE SHIP ANYWAY.

THERE. OKAY, I GUESS THAT'S IT...

WHAT ARE WE WAITING FOR?

27

day

VEIDT

Leo Winston
President
Marketing and Development

Dear Adrian,

   Even though you vetoed an expanded range of dolls based upon former advesaries, I still feel that the Ozymandias action figure line needs to attain a higher profile on the marketplace, and that to me indicates an extended range of product. Several possibilities have ocurred to me, outlined below.

   Firstly, figurines based upon Rorschach and Nite Owl seem to be viable. From a legal viewpoint, we're currently investigating the situation regarding the trademark and copyright laws. Our lawyers seem to think that since the costumed identities themselves are outlawed and illegal, there can be no legal claim to copyright upon their costumed images, leaving us free to register a copyright ourselves. This seems okay to me, but I'm advised that since you may have some personal connection with these individuals, there's a possibility that you'll feel differently.

   Secondly, the Moloch figurine. Since Edgar Jacobi died recently, there may be a question of taste, but from what our lawyers can determine, Jacobi left no estate likely to oppose such a marketing move. Also, once again there can be no legal claim on Jacobi's part concerning infringement of an identitiy which is illegal in the first place.

   Thirdly, and on a somewhat lighter note, I hope you will approve the inclusion of Bubastis. I know that she really didn't play any part in your exploits while you were an adventurer, but I understand that the people doing the Saturday morning Ozymandias cartoon show, scheduled for next fall, are keen that Bubastis should play a major role as a feline sidekick, making it therefore appropriate to play her up in our other merchandising.

   Anyway, in anticipation of your approval concerning this expansion of the line and in the absence of any immediate legal difficulties, I had some of the boys in production put together this dummy promotional leaflet. Hope you get a kick out of it, and I'll be calling next week to discuss the "Ziggurat of Death" role playing game, so we can discuss all this then.

   Best, as always,

   Leo Winston

   Leo Winston
   Marketing and Development

7

14

2

26

28

(OZ0001): Ozymandias:
This fully posable action doll, with removable cloak, tunic, and headband, is authentically molded to duplicate accurately the world-famous physique of athlete and former adventurer Adrian Veidt.

(OZ0002): Rorschach:
New Figure! Fully jointed and posable, this scale facsimile of the feared vigilante has a removable trenchcoat and hat.

(OZB001): Rorschach's Grappling Gun:
New Accessory! This scale model of the famous gas-powered grappling gun is spring loaded, and will fire a miniature hook, along with a length of line. Safe for children over five.

(OZ0003): Nite Owl:
New Figure! With removable cowl and belt, this fully posable model of the former nocturnal adventurer offers hours of exciting fun.

(OZB002): The Owlship:
New Accessory! Painstakingly assembled from existing photographs of this famous craft, our Owlship has an accessible and fully detailed cabin area, built to scale with **OZ0003**. Fully lighted cabin! Batteries not included.

(OZ0004): Moloch:
New Figure! With detachable handgun and stage magician's jacket, now you can thrill to the misdeeds of the infamous crown prince of the underworld in the safety of your own home.

(OZB003): Bubastis:
New Accessory! Fully posable, see the giant mutant Lynx of Ozymandias. Now she can help Adrian Veidt fight evil and help the innocent in *your* adventures, just like she does on TV.

Call.
Laurie
?s

Jeb—

Agree with you re: expansion of line. My study of recorded sales figures in a historical context suggests an increase in the sale of soldiers and action figures in times immediately prior to a period of anticipated war or bloodshed, and we should take advantage of this syndrome for as long as it lasts.

However, ethically very uncertain about Rorschach, Nite Owl and Moloch, plus accessories. Suggest instead we create costumed army of terrorists, introduce as main villains in Saturday cartoon, then duplicate here along with weapons, accessories and vehicles. More militaristic flavor will sell better. The American public has never really gone in for super-heroes in a big way. We'll discuss this next week.

Best,
Adrian Veidt

P.S.— Loved Bubastis. As soon as they're made, I must have one to give to her. Regards to Josephine and your children.

Oh, how the ghost of you clings...

Nostalgia by VEIDT

VEIDT Adrian Veidt
President and C.E.O.

THE VEIDT METHO

Hello. If you're reading
THAT, it's because you think you n
and magnetism? Advanced mental
we can offer you all these things
YOU! More than just a bodybuil
capable young men and women
difficult world that awaits in
understand, and if you follow i
results as a whole n

VEIDT Adrian Veidt
President and C.E.O.

Angela Neuberg
Director
Veidt Cosmetics & Toiletries

Dear Angela,
        Enclosed you'll find a representative sample of our current magazine and bill-
board advertising, promoting Nostalgia.
        The sexual imagery is obvious, the woman adjusting her stocking being overtly erot-
ic, yet layered with enough romantic ambiance to avoid offense. In our choice of models for
the Nostalgia ads I note that we have consistently chosen models with a slightly androgy-
nous quality to their beauty, which I presume is to afford us a window into the gay marketplace, a tendency more pronounced in the ads for Nostalgia aftershave. This is all well
and good, but it avoids the most significant element of the Nostalgia campaign:
        In the soft focus imagery and romantic atmosphere, the advertisements conjure an
idyllic picture of times past. It seems to me that the success of the campaign is directly
linked to the state of global uncertainty that has endured for the past forty years or more.
In an era of stress and anxiety, when the present seems unstable and the future unlikely,
the natural response is to retreat and withdraw from reality, taking recourse either in
fantasies of the future or in modified visions of a half-imagined past.
        While this marketing strategy is certainly relevant and indeed successful in a
context of social upheaval, I feel we must begin to take into account the fact that one
way or another, such conditions cannot endure indefinitely. Simply put, the current circumstances out civilization finds itself immersed in will either lead to war, or they won't.
If they lead to war, our best plans become irrelevant. If peace endures, I contend that a
new surge of social optimism is likely, necessitating a new image for Veidt cosmetics,
geared to a new consumer.
        To this end, starting next year we will begin to phase out the Nostalgia line of
ladies' and men's cosmetics, successful though they be, and replace them with a new line
that better exemplifies the spirit of our anticipated target group. This new line is to
be called the "Millenium" line. The imagery associated with it will be controversial and
modern, projecting a vision of a technological Utopia, a whole new universe of sensations
and pleasures that is just within reach.
        I would like the new line to be ready for launch in the summer, and would appre-
ciate it if some dummy ad copy and artwork could be assembled for my perusal and comment
sometime before Christmas.
        Anticipating your cooperation, and looking forward to working with you on this
one. My fondest regards to Frank. We must have lunch soon.
        Love,

        Adrian Veidt

ues

VEIDT **Adrian Veidt**
President and C.E.O.

Attached, manuscript for revised introduction
updated "Veidt Method" self-improvement booklet.
Please forward to relevant department.
—V.

THE VEIDT METHOD: AN INTRODUCTION

Hello. If you're reading this, it's because you sent away for my course, and if you did THAT, it's because you think you need a change in your life. A better body? Increased confidence and magnetism? Advanced mental techniques that will help you at home or in business? Well, yes, we can offer you all these things... but in order to have and enjoy them, there's got to be a new YOU! More than just a bodybuilding course, the Veidt Method is designed to produce bright and capable young men and women who will be fit to inherit the challenging, promising, and often difficult world that awaits in our future. The course is designed to, be easy to read and to understand, and if you follow it through, I can assure you that you and your friends will quickly notice the results as a whole new realm of ability and experience is opened up to you. Below is a brief summary of what you can expect to find in the later chapters of this volume.

UNDERSTANDING THE SELF
Both the body and the mind are parts of a biological robot that our immaterial souls inhabit. Like any machines, they can be tuned, improved and made to run more efficiently, as long as one understands the process for doing so. Through meditation and intellectual exercise, we may come to use our minds in ways that we never thought possible. In this first chapter of our manual we will discuss lateral thinking, Zen meditation, and the power of dreaming and the subconscious, along with other useful techniques for the advancement of the mind and intellect. Though not a religion, there are powerful spiritual disciplines behind the Veidt Method that must be understood if the student is to proceed.

HEALTH AND THE BODY
In our second chapter, we explore the connection between body and mind, and learn how this helps us to conquer pain and illness without recourse to drugs and medicines. We will show you, step by step, a number of techniques for focusing the mind's healing power upon any ailing part of the body. In relation to this, we also examine how the actions of the body can be used to aid and focus the mind, taking into account Yogic doctrines and martial training.

CREATING A NEW YOU
Our third and longest chapter presents a carefully coordinated series of physical and

intellectual exercise systems which, if followed correctly, can turn YOU into a superhuman, fully in charge of your own destiny. All that is required is the desire for perfection and the will to achieve it. No special equipment or other hidden cash extras are necessary. The Veidt Method paves the way for a bright and hopeful future in which anyone can be a hero.

YOU AND THE WORLD
Just as you are a whole organic being, complete unto yourself, so are you also part of a larger social organism consisting of the people around you, the people you work with, and ultimately the whole world. When you yourself are strong and healthy in mind and body, you will want to react in a healthy and positive way to the world around you, changing it for the better if you are able, and improving the lot of both yourself and your fellow man. Our final chapter will help you to understand the organism that is the world, and your part in it. You will learn that one can either surrender responsibility for one's actions to the rest of the social organism, to be pulled this way and that by society's predominating tensions, or that one can take control by flexing the muscles of the will common to us all, affecting our environment positively and responsibly.

So, in conclusion, welcome to the Veidt Method for physical fitness and self-improvement, a step by step guide to realizing exciting potentials latent within every one of us. I hope that you'll be intrigued by what you find within, and I know that if you persevere you'll walk away from this book a different person.
There's a bright new world just around the corner. It's going to need heroes just as badly as this one does, and one of them could be YOU!
All best wishes and encouragement,

Adrian Veidt

Adrian Veidt

CHAPTER XI

OBSERVATION=

MULTI-SCREEN VIEWING IS SEEMINGLY ANTICIPATED BY BURROUGHS' *CUT-UP* TECHNIQUE. HE SUGGESTED RE-ARRANGING WORDS AND IMAGES TO EVADE RATIONAL ANALYSIS, ALLOWING SUBLIMINAL HINTS OF THE *FUTURE* TO LEAK THROUGH...

AN IMPENDING WORLD OF EXOTICA, GLIMPSED ONLY PERIPHERALLY.

PERCEPTUALLY, THIS SIMULTANEOUS INPUT ENGAGES ME LIKE THE KINETIC EQUIVALENT OF AN ABSTRACT OR IMPRESSIONIST PAINTING...

PHOSPHOR-DOT SWIRLS JUXTAPOSE; MEANINGS COALESCE FROM SEMIOTIC CHAOS BEFORE REVERTING TO INCOHERENCE.

TRANSIENT AND ELUSIVE, THESE MUST BE GRASPED *QUICKLY:*

COMPUTER ANIMATIONS IMBUE EVEN *BREAKFAST CEREALS* WITH AN HALLUCIN-OGENIC FUTURITY; MUSIC CHANNELS PROCESS *INFOR-MATION-BLIPS*, AVOIDING LINEAR PRESENTATION, IMPLYING LIMITLESS PERSONAL CHOICE...

THESE REFERENCE POINTS ESTABLISHED, AN EMERGENT *WORLDVIEW* BECOMES GRADUALLY *DISCERNIBLE* AMIDST THE MEDIA'S *WHITE NOISE.*

THIS JIGSAW-FRAGMENT MODEL OF TOMORROW ALIGNS ITSELF PIECE BY PIECE, SPECIFIC AREAS NECESSARILY OBSCURED BY INDETERMINACY.

HOWEVER, BROAD ASSUMPTIONS REGARDING THIS POSTULATED FUTURE MAY BE DRAWN. WE CAN IMAGINE ITS *AMBIENCE.* WE CAN HYPOTHESIZE ITS *PSYCHOLOGY.*

IN CONJUNCTION WITH MASSIVE FORECASTED TECHNOLOGICAL ACCELERATION APPROACHING THE MILLENNIUM, THIS OBLIQUE AND SHIFTING CATHODE MOSAIC UNCOVERS THE BLUEPRINT FOR AN ERA OF NEW SENSATIONS AND POSSIBILITIES.

AN ERA OF THE CONCEIVABLE MADE *CONCRETE*...

...AND OF THE CASUALLY *MIRACULOUS.*

LOOK ON MY WORKS, YE MIGHTY

3

NOT COMING ANY FURTHER? NO?

FAIR ENOUGH. YOU WAIT THERE. THIS WON'T TAKE A MOMENT.

HELLO, MY FRIENDS. I'VE FINISHED MY WORK NOW, AND I'D BE HONORED IF THE THREE OF YOU WOULD JOIN ME FOR A SMALL DRINK IN THE *VIVARIUM*, BEFORE *DINNER.*

I HAVE SOMETHING TO CELEBRATE.

THANK YOU.

VEIDT OUT.

5

PARTYIN'! HOLOCAUST COMIN', GODDAMN KNOT-HEADS GOTTA PARTY! I CAN HEAR THAT GOD-FORBID-I-CALL-IT-MUSIC CLEAR FROM MADISON SQUARE!

YANG YANG YANG! MUSIC TO DROP BOMBS BY IS WHAT IT IS...

DAVIDSTOWN SLEPT, DESERTED SAVE FOR SILENCE.

TETHERING BOTH HORSES TO THE VERANDAH, I ENTERED MY FORMER RESIDENCE NOISE-LESSLY, CAREFUL NOT TO ROUSE THE BUTCHERS OCCUPYING IT FROM THEIR DEBAUCHED SLUMBER.

THEY'LL ALL COME OUT FIGHTIN' DRUNK, COVERED IN TATTOOS AND EAR-RINGS...

AN' IT'S RIGHT DOWN THE AVENUE! I TELL YA, THIS IS A BAD INTERSECTION. YOU NEVER KNOW WHAT'S GONNA TURN UP NEXT.

UNAWARE THAT DEATH WAS AMONGST THEM, THEY'D KNOW ITS DARK EMBRACE WITHOUT EVER UNDERSTANDING WHY.

ONE, HOWEVER, WAS AWAKE.

FRANTIC LEST HE SHOULD RAISE ALARUMS, I SET UPON HIM AS HE ENTERED THE NIGHT-WRAPPED CHAMBER.

IN FACT, I SEE ONE MORE STUPID HAIRCUT, I'M GONNA...

OH. HI. GETCHA SOMETHING?

NAH. GUESS JOSEPHINE POSTED THIS, LIKE SHE SAID. Y'KNOW, SOMETIMES SHE REALLY TRIES. SHE FINISHED WORK YET?

JOSEPHI...? OHH,...JOEY! YOU MUST BE HER... UH...

GIRL-FRIEND. EX. WE'VE BEEN FIGHTING.

IN CATARACT DARKNESS, I BLUDGEONED HIM, HIS SCREAMS UNNERVINGLY SHRILL.

OH. WELL, I AIN'T SEEN HER LATELY...

NO SWEAT. I'LL WAIT OUTSIDE THE PROMETHEAN. I'M NOT RELISHING THE ENCOUNTER.

NO PIRATES CAME, BUT SOMETHING WORSE. I LOOKED UP INTO FACES FAMILIAR SAVE FOR THEIR TERROR.

LISTEN, TELL HER HUSTLER'S DUE IN TOMORROW!

HUSTLER? GOD, IF IT'S OKAY, I'LL LET HER FIND OUT HERSELF.

THE CHILDREN WAILED. I LOOKED DOWN AT THE FIGURE BENEATH ME. THROUGH PUFFED AND BLOODIED LIPS SHE MOUTHED MY NAME.

HUH? WHADDI SAY? DON'T GO AWAY MAD...

THERE CAME AN UNDER-STANDING SO LARGE, IT LEFT NO ROOM FOR SANITY. AS I FLED PAST THE MOUNTED CADAVER OUTSIDE, LANTERNS FLARED IN NEARBY WINDOWS.

HUH! TIMES LIKE THESE, PEOPLE GOTTA BE HOSTILE? ME AN' ROSA SHOULDA QUIT THIS TOWN LIKE SHE WANNED, AN' ESCAPED FROM EVERYTHING.

I RAN, BUT THE KNOWLEDGE OF MY DAMNATION PACED ME, GLOATING, CELEBRATING ITS AWFUL VICTORY.

6

...ALTHOUGH TO UNCOVER THE REASONS FOR MY CURRENT ELATION, ONE NEED NOT DELVE QUITE SO DEEPLY INTO ANTIQUITY.

A MERE FORTY YEARS WILL SUFFICE, BACK TO MY CHILDHOOD.

"MY PARENTS REACHED AMERICA THE YEAR I WAS BORN, 1939.

"ENTERING SCHOOL, I WAS ALREADY EXCEPTIONALLY BRIGHT, MY PERFECT SCORES ON EARLY TEST PAPERS AROUSING SUCH SUSPICION THAT I CAREFULLY ACHIEVED ONLY AVERAGE GRADES THEREAFTER."

WHAT CAUSED SUCH PRECOCIOUSNESS? MY PARENTS WERE INTELLECTUALLY UNREMARKABLE, POSSESSING NO OBVIOUS GENETIC ADVANTAGES.

PERHAPS I DECIDED TO BE INTELLIGENT, RATHER THAN OTHERWISE? PERHAPS WE ALL MAKE SUCH DECISIONS, THOUGH THAT SEEMS A CALLOUS DOCTRINE.

"BY SEVENTEEN, MY PARENTS WERE BOTH DEAD AND I FACED A DIFFERENT DECISION.

"MY INHERITANCE OFFERED LIFE-LONG IDLE LUXURY, AND YET, NEEDING NOTHING, I BURNED WITH THE PARADOXICAL URGE TO DO EVERYTHING.

"DO YOU UNDERSTAND?"

MY INTELLECT SET ME APART. FACED WITH DIFFICULT CHOICES, I KNEW NOBODY WHOSE ADVICE MIGHT PROVE USEFUL. NOBODY LIVING.

THE ONLY HUMAN BEING WITH WHOM I FELT ANY KINSHIP DIED THREE HUNDRED YEARS BEFORE THE BIRTH OF CHRIST.

VEIDT

"ALEXANDER OF MACEDONIA. I IDOLIZED HIM. A YOUNG ARMY COMMANDER, HE'D SWEPT ALONG THE COASTS OF TURKEY AND PHOENICIA, SUBDUING EGYPT BEFORE TURNING HIS ARMIES TOWARDS PERSIA...

"HE DIED, AGED THIRTY-THREE, RULING MOST OF THE CIVILIZED WORLD."

RULING WITHOUT BARBARISM! AT ALEXANDRIA, HE INSTITUTED THE ANCIENT WORLD'S GREATEST SEAT OF LEARNING.

TRUE, PEOPLE DIED...PERHAPS UNNECESSARILY, THOUGH WHO CAN JUDGE SUCH THINGS? YET HOW NEARLY HE APPROACHED HIS VISION OF A UNITED WORLD!

"I WAS DETERMINED TO MEASURE MY SUCCESS AGAINST HIS. FIRSTLY, I GAVE AWAY MY INHERITANCE TO DEMONSTRATE THE POSSIBILITY OF ACHIEVING ANYTHING, STARTING FROM NOTHING.

"NEXT I DEPARTED FOR NORTHERN TURKEY, TO RETRACE MY HERO'S STEPS."

I WANTED TO MATCH HIS ACCOMPLISHMENT, BRINGING AN AGE OF ILLUMINATION TO A BENIGHTED WORLD.

HEH.

I WANTED TO HAVE SOMETHING TO SAY TO HIM, SHOULD WE MEET IN THE HALL OF LEGENDS.

8

9

"I FOLLOWED THE PATH OF ALEX-
ANDER'S WAR MACHINE ALONG THE
BLACK SEA COAST, IMAGINING HIS
ARMIES TAKING PORT AFTER PORT;
ANCIENT BLOOD ON ANCIENT BRONZE.

"STRANGELY, BEFORE SUBDUING
PHOENICIA, HE STRUCK NORTH
TOWARDS GORDIUM..."

...PERHAPS BECAUSE
OF THE CHALLENGE
IT PRESENTED: THE
ANCIENT WORLD'S
GREATEST PUZZLE
WAS THERE, A
KNOT THAT
COULDN'T BE
UNTIED.

ALEXANDER
CUT IT IN
TWO WITH HIS
SWORD.

LATERAL
THINKING, YOU
SEE. CENTURIES
AHEAD OF HIS
TIME.

"HEADING SOUTH, HE ENTERED
EGYPT THROUGH MEMPHIS, WHERE
THEY PROCLAIMED HIM SON OF
AMON, JUDGE OF THE DEAD, WHOSE
NAME MEANS 'THE HIDDEN ONE'.

"UNDER RULE FROM ALEXANDRIA, THE
CLASSIC CULTURE OF THE GREAT
PHARAOHS WAS RESTORED."

I FOLLOWED
HIM THROUGH
BABYLON, UP THROUGH
KABUL TO SAMARKHAND,
THEN DOWN THE INDUS,
WHERE HE FIRST
MET ELEPHANTS-
OF-WAR.

WHERE HE'D
TURNED BACK
TO QUELL DISSENT
AT HOME, I TRAVELLED
ON, THROUGH CHINA
AND TIBET, GATHERING
MARTIAL WISDOM
AS I WENT.

"ALEXANDER RETURNED TO BABYLON
TO DIE OF AN INFECTION, AGED
THIRTY-THREE. AMONGST ITS
RUINED ZIGGURATS, I SAW AT
LAST HIS FAILINGS...

"HE'D NOT UNITED ALL THE
WORLD, NOR BUILT A UNITY
THAT WOULD SURVIVE HIM."

DISILLUSIONED
BUT DETERMINED
TO COMPLETE
MY ODYSSEY, I
FOLLOWED HIS
CORPSE TO ITS
RESTING PLACE IN
ALEXANDRIA.

THE NIGHT BEFORE
RETURNING TO
AMERICA, I
WANDERED INTO
THE DESERT AND
ATE A BALL OF
HASHISH I'D
BEEN GIVEN
IN TIBET.

"THE ENSUING VISION TRANSFORMED
ME. WADING THROUGH POWDERED
HISTORY, I HEARD DEAD KINGS
WALKING UNDERGROUND; HEARD
FANFARES SOUND THROUGH
HUMAN SKULLS.

"ALEXANDER HAD MERELY
RESURRECTED AN AGE
OF PHARAOHS. THEIR
WISDOM, TRULY IMMORTAL,
NOW INSPIRED ME!"

10

12

MANNERS.

17

WAS HE *REHEARSING* IT, PERHAPS, AS THE *MOTORCADE* REACHED THE *PLAZA*...

...NEVER SUSPECTING THAT ON THE WALLS OF WORLD *TYRANNY*, CROSS-HAIRS WATCHED *HIM*.

"WE ALL REALIZED THEN HOW *BAD* THINGS WERE. I CONTINUED *AD-VENTURING*, BUT IT SEEMED *HOLLOW*.

"I FOUGHT ONLY THE *SYMPTOMS*, LEAVING THE *DISEASE* ITSELF *UNCHECKED*."

I DESPISED MYSELF; MY SHAM *CRUSADE*. KNOWING MANKIND'S PROBLEMS, I'D *BLINDED* MYSELF TO THEM.

I FELT *HELPLESS* AGAINST FORCES GREATER THAN ANY I'D *ANTICIPATED*.

"TOO *COWARDLY* TO *CONFRONT* MY *ANXIETIES*, I HAD LIFE'S BLACK COMEDY EXPLAINED TO ME BY THE COMEDIAN HIMSELF AT THE *CRIMEBUSTERS* FIASCO IN '66.

"I'M SURE YOU *REMEMBER*."

HE DISCUSSED NUCLEAR WAR'S *INEVITABILITY*; DESCRIBED MY FUTURE ROLE AS "SMARTEST GUY ON THE CINDER"...

...AND OPENED MY *EYES*. ONLY THE *BEST* COMEDIANS ACCOMPLISH *THAT*.

"I REMEMBER THE *CHARRED MAP* BETWEEN MY *FINGERS*; NELSON SAYING 'SOMEONE'S GOT TO SAVE THE WORLD', HIS TREMULOUS, COMPLAINING VOICE...

"THAT'S WHEN I UNDERSTOOD."

THAT'S WHEN IT HIT ME.

"CONSOLING NELSON, I *LEFT*. OUTSIDE, BLAKE ARGUED WITH *LAURIE* AND HER MOTHER.

"I SWORE TO DENY HIS KIND THEIR LAST BLACK LAUGH AT EARTH'S EXPENSE."

I *ALSO* SWORE THAT WHEN NEXT I MET *BLAKE* OR ANY *OTHER* FOE, THOUGH PERHAPS NOT ON MY *TERRITORY*...

...IT WOULD CERTAINLY BE ON MY *TERMS*.

19

HI. FANCY MEETING YOU HERE.

GLORIA?

I KNEW YOU CAME THIS WAY *HOME*, SO I FIGURED I'D MEET YOU FROM *WORK*. I'M NOT READY TO VISIT BACK AT THE *APARTMENT* JUST YET.

"JUST YET"?

Panel 3:
WELL, I *WANT* TO COME BACK. I *MISS* YOU, MALCOLM. I *MISS* THE PERSON YOU *WERE*...

...BUT I CAN'T LIVE WITH SOMEONE WHO FEELS DRIVEN TO HELP *HOPELESS CASES*, THEN LETS *THEIR* MISERY AFFECT *OUR* LIVES.

Panel 4:
IF YOU CAN PROMISE ME YOU'LL ASK FOR A TRANSFER TO DIFFERENT WORK WITH DIFFERENT *PATIENTS*, I CAN COME HOME... IF THAT'S WHAT YOU *WANT*.

GLORIA, OF *COURSE* THAT'S WHAT I WANT, BUT, UH...

Panel 5:
WELL, *DO* IT! I'M NOT GOING TO SHARE YOU WITH A WORLD FULL OF *SCREW-UPS* AND *MANIC DEPRESSIVES*. I'M NOT GOING TO SHARE MY LIFE WITH THEM.

MALCOLM? MALCOLM, ARE YOU *LISTENING* TO ME?

GLORIA, I'M SORRY ...THOSE *PEOPLE*... THEY'RE *HURTING* EACH OTHER...

MALCOLM? DON'T YOU *DARE!* DON'T YOU *DARE* GET INVOLVED!

DIDN'T YOU LISTEN TO A WORD I JUST *SAID*?

Panel 7:
GLORIA, PLEASE. I *HAVE* TO. IN A WORLD LIKE *THIS*...

I MEAN, IT'S ALL WE *CAN* DO, TRY TO *HELP* EACH OTHER. IT'S ALL THAT *MEANS* ANY-THING...

PLEASE. PLEASE UNDER-STAND.

Panel 8:
MALCOLM, I'M *WARNING* YOU! YOU LET YOUR-SELF GET DRAWN TOWARDS ANOTHER HEAP OF SOME-BODY ELSE'S *GRIEF*, I DON'T WANT TO *SEE* YOU AGAIN!

GLORIA ...I'M *SORRY*. IT'S THE *WORLD*...

Panel 9:
I CAN'T *RUN* FROM IT.

ITS DARK AND LURCHING MASS FILLED ALL MY VISION. I SAW THE HEADS NAILED TO ITS PROW, HEARD DRUNKEN LAUGHTER; ENCOURAGEMENTS BARKED FROM THE DECKS ABOVE...

CLOSER, IT CAME.

CLOSER.

20

BRUTALLY, I'D BEEN BROUGHT NOSE TO NOSE WITH MANKIND'S *MORTALITY*; THE DREADFUL, IRREFUTABLE *FACT* OF IT.

FOR THE FIRST TIME, I GENUINELY UNDERSTOOD THAT EARTH MIGHT *DIE*. I RECOGNIZED THE *FRAGILITY* OF OUR WORLD IN INCREASINGLY HAZARDOUS TIMES...

... AND YET WHAT COULD I *DO*?

MY *FIRST* STEP WAS TO STAND BACK AS FAR AS I COULD, TO VIEW THE PROBLEM FROM A FRESH *PERSPECTIVE*, MY *VISTA* WIDENING WITH MY *COMPREHENSION*.

I SAW *EAST* AND *WEST*, LOCKED INTO AN ESCALATING *ARMS SPIRAL*, THEIR MUTUAL TERROR AND SUSPICION MOUNTING WITH THE *MISSILES*, MAKING THE POSSIBILITY OF DISARMAMENT PROGRESSIVELY MORE *REMOTE*.

GRADUALLY, I CLOSED UPON THE *HEART* OF THE DILEMMA.

HERE WAS A *KNOT* TO TRY EVEN *ALEXANDER'S* INGENUITY.

BOTH SIDES *REALIZED* THE SUICIDAL *IMPLICATIONS* OF NUCLEAR CONFLICT, YET COULDN'T STOP RACING *TOWARDS* IT LEST THEIR *OPPONENTS* SHOULD *OVERTAKE* THEM.

AFRAID OF THEIR *WEAPONS*, AFRAID OF *LOSING* THEM, AFRAID TO *BLINK* OR TURN THEIR *BACKS*...

MEANWHILE, EXPENSIVE ARSENALS MEANT LESS CASH TO SPEND UPON THEIR *OLD*; THEIR *SICK* AND *HOMELESS*; ON THEIR *CHILDREN'S* EDUCATIONS.

AS STOCKPILES *GREW*, AS *COMPUTERS* REDUCED HUMAN *INVOLVEMENT*, THE SPECTRE OF *ACCIDENTAL APOCALYPSE* STALKED EVER *CLOSER*.

SIMPLY GIVEN THE *MATHEMATICS* OF THE SITUATION, SOONER OR LATER *CONFLICT* WOULD BE INEVITABLE!

HOWEVER, WITHOUT A PRACTICAL *SOLUTION* AT HAND, WHAT USE WAS IT TO SUDDENLY NOTICE THE *PERILS* OF THE SITUATION?

SIMILARLY A *SOLUTION* WOULD BE *EQUALLY* USELESS ...

...UNLESS ONE POSSESSED THE *MUSCLE* TO BACK IT UP; THE BRUTE *POWER* TO SEE ONE'S WILL *IMPLEMENTED*.

I TOOK ANOTHER STEP BACK, AND THOUGHT AGAIN.

21

OTHER FACTORS EMERGED: ARMS EXPENDITURES BOOSTED INTERNATIONAL LENDING RATES. TO REPAY SOARING DEBT INTEREST, NATIONS LIKE BRAZIL LEVELLED THEIR FORESTS.

NUCLEAR POWER, PROVIDING VITAL WEAPONS-GRADE WASTE, BECAME MANDATORY.

WAR ASIDE, ATOMIC DEADLOCK GUIDED US DOWNHILL TOWARDS ENVIRONMENTAL RUIN.

JON'S PRESENCE ACCELERATED THIS, THOUGH LESS THAN YOU'D IMAGINE. ANY SIGNIFICANT POWER IMBALANCE WOULD YIELD SIMILAR RESULTS.

NEVERTHELESS, HE SOMEHOW SYMBOLIZED MANKIND'S PROBLEMS. AS TENSIONS ROSE, THE ELEVATION OF COSTUMED HEROES BECAME A DESCENT...

I FORE-SAW THAT BY THE LATE SEVENTIES, IT WOULD REACH BOTTOM.

THIS LEFT TEN YEARS TO BUILD A FORTUNE AND REPUTATION TO SUSTAIN ME BEYOND THAT POINT, ALLOWING ME THE POWER AND LEVER-AGE I'D SURELY NEED.

DEVELOPING THE BASIC PATENT FOR PUBLIC SPARK HYDRANTS, I FINANCED DIMENSIONAL DEVELOPMENTS WITH THE PROCEEDS.

MY PLAN REQUIRED PREPARATION FOR THE DAY WHEN I'D ASSUME THE ASPECT OF KINGLY RAMESES, LEAVING ALEXANDER THE ADVENTURER AND HIS TRAPPINGS TO GATHER DUST.

EACH STEP HAD TO BE TAKEN CAREFULLY, CONSTANTLY STRIVING TO KEEP IN MIND THE ENORMOUS SCALE OF WHAT WAS AT STAKE!

THE EARTH. HUMANITY. ALL WE'VE EVER KNOWN...

"END OF THE WORLD" DOES THE CONCEPT NO JUSTICE.

THE WORLD'S PRESENT WOULD END. ITS FUTURE, IMMEASURABLY VASTER, WOULD ALSO VANISH.

EVEN OUR PAST WOULD BE CANCELLED. OUR STRUGGLE FROM THE PRIMAL OOZE, EVERY CHILDBIRTH, EVERY PERSONAL SACRIFICE REND-ERED MEANINGLESS, LEADING ONLY TO DUST, TOSSED ON THE VOID-WINDS.

SAVE FOR RICHARD NIXON, WHOSE NAME ADORNS A PLAQUE UPON THE MOON, NO HUMAN VESTIGE WOULD REMAIN.

RUINS BECOME SAND, SAND BLOWS AWAY... ALL OUR RICHNESS AND COLOR AND BEAUTY WOULD BE LOST...

...AS IF IT HAD NEVER BEEN.

22

THE WORLD I'D TRIED TO SAVE WAS LOST BEYOND RECALL. I WAS A HORROR: AMONGST HORRORS MUST I DWELL.

A ROPE SNAKED DOWN SPLUTTERING, I GRABBED IT...

SEE, PEOPLE DON'T REACH OUT AND MAKE CONTACT.

...AND FROM THE DECKS ABOVE A CHEER WENT UP, BOTH GROSS AND BLACK, ITS STENCH AFFRONTING HEAVEN.

THE END.

THAT'S WHY THERE'S THIS COMMOTION ALL THE TIME, THIS CONFLICT. PEOPLE DON'T CONNECT WITH EACH OTHER.

Panel 3:
IT'S LIKE, YOU BEEN COMING HERE WEEKS, READIN' THAT JUNK OVER AN' OVER, AN' YET WE AIN'T EXACTLY CLOSE...

'CAUSE THEY DON'T MAKE SENSE, MAN! THAT'S WHY I GOTTA READ 'EM OVER.

Panel 4:
THAT AIN'T THE POINT.

LISTEN, WHEN MY ROSA DIED, MOST OF OUR FRIENDS WERE HER FRIENDS: THEY STOPPED CALLING. I TOOK THIS JOB TO MEET PEOPLE, Y'KNOW?

SO...WHAT'S YOUR NAME? WHADDAYA DOIN' HERE?

Panel 5:
MY NAME'S BERNIE. I'M HERE BECAUSE MY MOM'S WORKING, AN' MY SISTER, SHE'S OUT TOO, AND THESE HYDRANTS ARE WARM, Y'KNOW?

BERNIE? SHORT FOR BERNARD? WELL I'LL BE HORSEWHIPPED! THAT'S MY NAME!

SO? AIN'T NO BIG DEAL. LOTTA PEOPLE CALLED BERNARD, MAN. DON'T SIGNIFY FOR NOTHIN'.

WELL, SURE, BUT... WAIT A MINUTE. WHAT THE HELL'S GOING ON...?

Panel 7:
FIGHT. PULL OVER.

STEVE, YOU JUST GOT SUSPENDED. THIS AIN'T YOUR PROBLEM. SOME OTHER UNIT CAN HANDLE IT.

I'M STILL ME, JOE. PULL HER OVER.

Panel 8:
AW SHIT...

LISTEN, MILO, YOU LEAVE WORK EARLY FOR A BEER WITH YOUR BROTHER, BUSINESS AIN'T GONNA COLLAPSE.

NO, BUT... HEY... POLICE. WHAT'S HAPPENING?

Panel 9:
THAT'S JOEY! THAT'S ONE OF MY DRIVERS, IN A FIGHT...

HELL! ANOTHER MINUTE, WE'D HAVE BEEN GONE.

TALK ABOUT LOUSY TIMING!

EACH STEP WAS SYNCHRONIZED.

JON, BEING TOO *POWERFUL* AND *UNPREDICTABLE* TO FIT MY *PLANS,* NEEDED *REMOVING.* THUS, DIMENSIONAL DEVELOPMENTS HIRED HIS PAST *ASSOCIATES...*

...AND GAVE THEM *CANCER?*

YES. WEAVER FIRST, SLATER AND MOLOCH *LATER.* UNWITTINGLY EXPOSED TO *RADIATION,* THEY WERE CLOSELY *OBSERVED,* CULTIVATED AS WEAPONS AGAINST *JON.*

MEANWHILE, TAKING ADVANTAGE OF NEW *TECHNOLOGY,* I RESEARCHED *GENETICS...* BUBASTIS WAS AN EARLY *SUCCESS...* AND *TELEPORTATION.*

SINCE JON PROVED *TELEPORTATION POSSIBLE,* WHY DEVELOP ELECTRIC *CARS?* MY *RESEARCHES* WERE *VITAL...* LIKE MY *ISLAND,* SECRETLY PURCHASED IN 1970.

THE ONLY HERO RETAINING PUBLIC *SYMPATHY,* I QUIT TWO YEARS BEFORE THE *KEENE ACT,* CONCENTRATING ON MY *PLAN.*

"UNABLE TO UNITE THE WORLD BY *CONQUEST...* ALEXANDER'S METHOD ...I WOULD *TRICK* IT; FRIGHTEN IT TOWARDS SALVATION WITH HISTORY'S GREATEST *PRACTICAL JOKE.*"

"THAT'S WHAT UPSET THE *COMEDIAN,* WHEN AWARENESS OF MY SCHEME CRASHED *IN* UPON HIM:"

"PROFESSIONAL *JEALOUSY.*"

BLAKE'S *MURDER.* YOU *CONFESS?*

CONFESSION IMPLIES *PENITENCE.* I MERELY REGRET HIS ACCIDENTAL *INVOLVEMENT.*

RETURNING FROM *NICARAGUA* BY *AIR,* HE SPOTTED A *SHIP* DOCKING AT AN UN-CHARTED *ISLAND.* SUSPECTING SANDINISTA BASES, HE RESOLVED TO *INVESTIGATE.*

"I *PICTURE* HIM, SWIMMING TO THE *ISLAND,* DAGGER IN *TEETH,* PENETRATING ITS *INSTALLATIONS.* WHAT HE *FOUND* MUST HAVE COME AS A TERRIBLE *BLOW.*"

"IMAGINE... THE PERFECT *FIGHTING MAN* DISCOVER-ING A PLOT TO PUT AN END TO *WAR...*"

"...AN END TO *FIGHTING.*"

INSTITUTE FOR EXTRASPATIAL STUDIES

24

AFTER **BLAKE**, I NEUTRALIZED **JON**. STOLEN **PSYCHIATRIC REPORTS** INDICATED HIS MENTAL **WITHDRAWAL**. THE **CANCER ALLEGATIONS** MADE IT **PHYSICAL**.

BY THEN, RORSCHACH'S **MASK KILLER** HUNT NEEDED STOPPING. MY **OWN** "ASSASSINATION," CONFIRMING HIS ERRONEOUS THEORY, PLACED ME **BEYOND SUSPICION**.

"I'D HIRED MY OWN KILLER THROUGH A THIRD **PARTY**. WHEN I FED HIM THE **CYANIDE CAPSULE**, PERHAPS HE **REALIZED** THIS.

"I KNEW ONLY **TRIUMPH**... **NOTHING** NOW STOOD BETWEEN **ME** AND MY **GOAL**. HUMANITY'S **FATE** RESTED SAFELY IN MY **HANDS**."

ADRIAN, THIS IS **CRAZY**. WHO'D BELIEVE AN ALIEN **INVASION**?

HITLER SAID PEOPLE SWALLOW LIES **EASILY**, PROVIDED THEY'RE **BIG** ENOUGH. I PLANNED TO BUILD MY **MONSTER**, TELEPORT IT TO A CERTAIN **DESTINATION**...

SAID TELEPORTATION UNWORKABLE.

"IT WORKS **FINE**, ASSUMING YOU **WANT** THINGS TO EXPLODE ON **ARRIVAL**.

"TELEPORTED TO **NEW YORK**, MY CREATURE'S **DEATH** WOULD TRIGGER MECHANISMS WITHIN ITS MASSIVE **BRAIN**, CLONED FROM A HUMAN **SENSITIVE**...

"...THE RESULTANT PSYCHIC **SHOCKWAVE** KILLING HALF THE **CITY**."

ADRIAN, I'M **SORRY**...YOU NEED **HELP**. I KNOW THIS "**HALF NEW YORK**" STUFF IS BULLSHIT, BUT I'M **STILL** GLAD WE GOT HERE BEFORE YOU GOT DEEPER **INTO** THIS MESS.

CHRIST, YOU SERIOUSLY **PLANNED** ALL THIS **MAD SCIENTIST** STUFF?

"I MEAN, WHEN WAS THIS HOPELESS BLACK FANTASY SUPPOSED TO **HAPPEN**?

"WHEN WERE YOU PLANNING TO **DO** IT?"

26

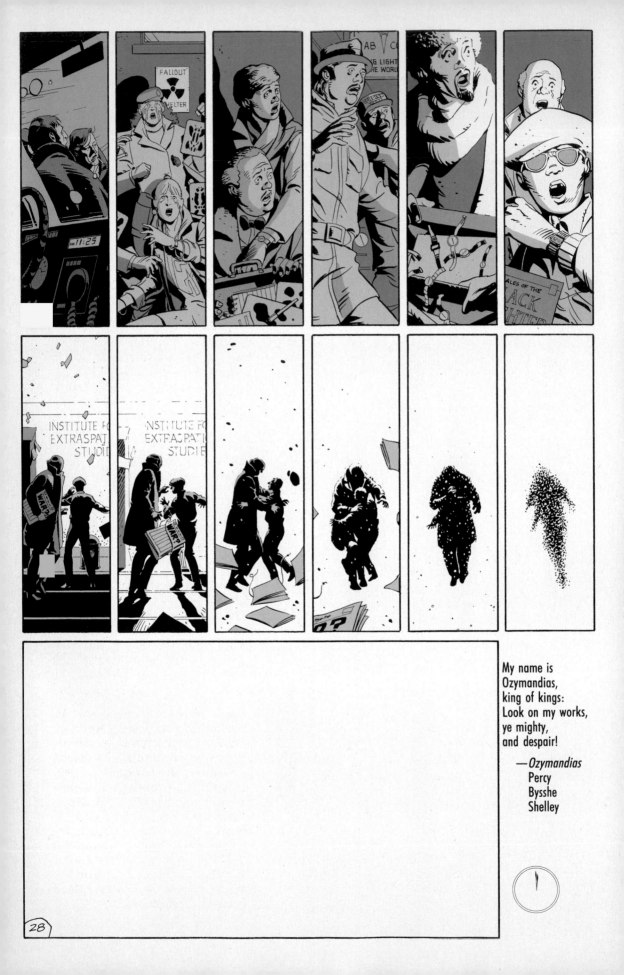

My name is
Ozymandias,
king of kings:
Look on my works,
ye mighty,
and despair!

—*Ozymandias*
Percy
Bysshe
Shelley

AFTER THE MASQUERADE:

Superstyle and the art of humanoid watching.

DOUG ROTH VISITS ANTARCTICA TO INTERVIEW ADRIAN VEIDT

VEIDT: "The frightening thing about the campaign to re-elect the president is that in the wake of the victory in Vietnam, I don't see how they can fail. C.R.E.E.P.! What a terrible acronym. I wonder who coined that one? Somebody who watched too many 'Man From U.N.C.L.E.' episodes in the sixties ... Liddy, or one of those other Washington humanoids."

"Humanoids." I'm sitting talking with a retired superhero in a glass dome filled with tropical flowers and hummingbirds, while outside the antarctic wind builds snowdrifts against the glass. I would imagine myself beyond surprise by this point, yet the sudden use of such an odd term is startling. Have I detected a hitherto unnoticed contempt for mere humans behind that eminently likable golden facade? Why "humanoids"? I put this to him, and he chuckles.

VEIDT: "I'm sorry, it's a sort of one-man private joke. I've been referring to Nixon's close subordinates as humanoids since I heard about the banquet ... and this is true, I promise ... where one of the presidential aides spilled a glass of water over Vice-President Ford. The aide was incredibly apologetic, obviously, but Ford just smiled and said 'Oh, that's okay. Nobody's human.' (*Laughter*) I've called 'em humanoids ever since."

Continued

The laughter of Adrian Veidt is deep and rich, filled with a warmth I hadn't anticipated as the jet he'd arranged lowered me gently from the blank white antarctic sky towards the dangerously small-looking black hyphen of the landing strip, set into the endless pack ice far below. The landscape was hard and cold, too big to get to grips with, and I expected much the same of any man who'd choose to live in it.

The plane was met at the landing strip by three enthusiastically friendly Vietnamese men who led me between obelisks of dark marble with rolling purple highlights towards the fortress dominating the nude white reaches beyond.

Servants? My liberal sensibilities recoiled at the concept with a predictable knee-jerk. Later, however, on learning that the men had been Vietcong refugees in danger of losing their lives in the purges following America's victory without Veidt's intervention, I wasn't so sure. Since Antarctica is owned by no nation, the men are theoretically safe from extradition, and their nominal boss seems to treat them more as respected friends than as lackeys. Certainly, they themselves seem deliriously happy with both their lot and their landlord.

"Mr. Veidt has made the effort to understand our culture. He talks to us often concerning our religious beliefs, asking many questions." The man who tells me this is sincere and heartfelt in his testimonial, showing an almost fatherly protective anxiety that this magazine should not misrepresent his employer:

"He is not one of your pop music stars. He does not inject drugs, or treat young women badly. Make sure that you say that."

When we reach the fortress, Veidt is still completing his daily workout in a gymnasium of vast, almost dreamlike proportions, where parallel bars meet at infinity. I'm cordially invited to watch while he finishes up, and as I observe that perfect swiss-watch of a body twirling and circling above me in easy defiance of gravity, all my earlier doubts concerning Veidt's accessibility return.

There he is, right up there above me: the man. Adrian Veidt. Ozyman . . . whoops. Uh-uh. We don't call him that anymore, do we? The mask is gone, but as he loops the high bar in slow, graceful centrifuge he still wears the golden leotard, and the headband. Every girlfriend I've had in the past four years has wanted to lay this guy, more than Jagger, more than Springsteen or D'Eath or any of those also-rans, and now here I am, squinting up at him, and yes, goddamn it, I have to goddamned admit that he looks like a goddamned god! I can't quite believe he'll submit to being interviewed by someone so obviously mired in the dregs of the gene pool as myself . . .

. . . but here he comes, dropping to the floor, picking up the purple towel that I realize later is actually the tunic of his costume, and wiping himself beneath the arms with it in a distinctly Homo sapiens fashion. He's walking towards me, his smile somewhere between Jackie Coogan and J.F.K., sticking out a hand that grips mine strongly enough to make me glad it's friendly. He glances towards the gymnasium windows, outside which a blizzard seems to be commencing and smiles again.

"Not the sort of snow you're used to in California, Mr. Roth."

A coke joke! Adrian Veidt, Ozy-freakin'-mandias himself has just told me a _coke joke!_ Whoooo-ee! We fall easily into conversation from that point on, and after he's dressed he takes me for a tour of his fortress, opulent beyond the wildest dreams of Versailles. We end up in a large section of the main hall where one wall appears to be entirely covered with TV screens, all tuned to different channels. It is here that we hold our interview, and I notice his eyes often drifting across the riot of clashing images as we speak. It's only after I express worries concerning background noise and my recording equipment that he thinks to turn the sound of the multiple televisions down. They don't seem to affect _his_ concentration at all.

Before launching into my interview spiel, I take a breath and remember why I'm here. Almost lost in the cacophony surrounding the old Trickster's Constitutional amendment scam, one of America's best-respected and most consistently left-leaning superheroes quietly retired from crimefighting to pursue a career in business. When this magazine phoned him to ask why, he kindly offered to fly me up to his antarctic retreat where we could conduct the interview in comfort. Exhaling, I press the record button and begin.

NOVA: So, how do you get to be a superhero? Were your parents rich? I mean, did that give you advantages?

VEIDT: No more than I could help. My mother left me a lot of money when she died, but I gave it to charity when I was seventeen. I wanted to prove that I could accomplish anything I wanted starting from absolutely nothing. Also, I wanted to free myself of concern for money. Consequently, it's never been a problem for me. To answer your question, you get to be a superhero by believing in the hero within you and summoning him or her forth by an act of will. Believing in yourself and your own potential is the first step to realizing that potential. Alternatively, you could do as Jon did: Fall into a nuclear reactor and hope for the best. On the whole, I think I prefer to stick to my own methods. (_Laughter_)

NOVA: You'll forgive me for saying so, but isn't that philosophy a little Norman Vincent Peale? That self-realization stuff? How exactly do you exploit that potential to the degree that you obviously have?

VEIDT: The disciplines of physical exercise, meditation and study aren't terribly esoteric. The means to attain a capability far beyond that of the so-called ordinary person are within reach of everyone, if their desire and their will are strong enough. I have studied science, art, religion and a hundred different philosophies. Anyone could do as much. By applying what you learn and ordering your thoughts in an intelligent manner it is possible to accomplish almost anything. Possible for the "ordinary person." There's a notion I'd like to see buried: the ordinary person. Ridiculous. There is no ordinary person.

NOVA: Returning to your costumed career, why did you quit?

VEIDT: There were a number of reasons, but I suppose basically it boiled down to my increasing uncertainty about the role of the costumed hero in the seventies. What does fighting crime mean, exactly? Does it mean upholding the law when a woman shoplifts to feed her children, or does it mean struggling to uncover the ones who, quite legally, have brought about her poverty? Yes, I've busted drug rings and been accused of being an establishment pawn for doing so . . . that happened a lot in the sixties. I've also uncovered plots by breakaway extremist factions within the Pentagon, for example the plot to release some unpleasantly specific diseases upon the population of Africa, the exposure of which led to the *New Frontiersman* denouncing me as a "Puppet of Peking" on the strength of my youthful travels through the East. I guess I've just reached a point where I've started to wonder whether all the grandstanding and fighting individual evils does

much good for the world as a whole. Those evils are just symptoms of an overall sickness of the human spirit, and I don't believe you can cure a disease by suppressing its symptoms. That whole *Contac-400* approach to our society's problems, I despair of it. It doesn't work. Maybe as a businessman I can do more good, on a more meaningful scale.

NOVA: What sort of world do you see it being, in the future?

VEIDT: That depends upon us . . . each and every one of us. Futurology interests me perhaps more than any other single subject, and as such I devote a great deal of time to its study. Even so, technology is progressing at an ever-accelerating pace, and by early next century I would hesitate to predict *any* limitations upon what we might be capable of. I would say without hesitation that a new world is within our grasp, filled with unimaginable experiences and possibilities, if only we want it badly enough. Not a utopia . . . I don't believe that any species could continue to grow and keep from stagnation without *some* adversity . . . but a society with a more human basis, where the problems that beset us are at least *new* problems.

NOVA: You don't think there's a possibility we may have damaged the environment beyond repair, or that we might someday have a fatal nuclear showdown with the Soviets?

Continued

Veidt cont.

VEIDT: Of course. Of course I do. I'd be ignoring the facts if I didn't accept those things as strong possibilities. As I said, it all depends on us, on whether we, individually, want Armageddon or a new world of fabulous, limitless potential. That's not such an obvious question as it seems. I believe there are some people who really do want, if only subconsciously, an end to the world. They want to be spared the responsibilities of maintaining that world, to be spared the effort of imagination needed to realize such a future. And of course, there are other people who want very much to live. I see twentieth century society as a sort of race between enlightenment and extinction. In one lane you have the four horsemen of the apocalypse . . .

NOVA: . . . and in the other?

VEIDT: The seventh cavalry. (*Laughter*)

NOVA: Changing the subject entirely, do you listen to much music? I wondered what your tastes might be, as a superhero . . .

VEIDT: I like electronic music. That's a very superhero-ey thing to like, I suppose, isn't it? I like avant-garde music in general. Cage, Stockhausen, Penderecki, Andrew Lang, Pierre Henry. Terry Riley is very good. Oh, and I've heard some interesting new music from Jamaica . . . a sort of hybrid between electronic music and reggae. It's a fascinating study in the new musical forms generated when a largely pre-technological culture is given access to modern recording techniques without the technological preconceptions that we've allowed to accumulate, limiting our vision. It's called dub music. You'd like it, I'm sure.

NOVA: How do you get on with the rest of the superhero fraternity? Some of them seem very right-wing in contrast with your own stance. I'm thinking of Rorschach, the Comedian, Dr. Manhattan . . .

VEIDT: *Jon*? Right-wing? (*Laughs*) If there's one thing in this cosmos that that man *isn't* capable of doing it's having a political bias. Believe me . . . you have to meet him to understand. I mean, which do you prefer, red ants or black ants?

NOVA: Uh . . .? Well, I don't have any particular preference . . .

VEIDT: Exactly. Well, imagine how Jon feels. Rorschach, I don't know very well. I believe he's a man of great integrity, but he seems to see the world in very black and white, Manichean terms. I personally believe that to be an intellectual limitation.

NOVA: And the Comedian? I understand there's no love lost between you. I heard that he beat you in combat, back when you were just starting out . . .

VEIDT: Yes, well, that was a case of mistaken identity and general misunderstanding. For some reason it happens a lot when costumed crime-fighters meet for the first time. (*Laughter*)

NOVA: But you and the Comedian don't like each other?

VEIDT: My, but you're determined, aren't you? (*Laughs*) No, we're not great friends. It's largely a political difference. He sees me as an intellectual dilettante dabbling in national affairs that don't concern me. I see him as an amoral mercenary allying himself to whichever political faction seems likely to grant him the greatest license. The difference is as simple and as profound as that.

NOVA: There's no general sense of disillusionment with your fellow crimefighters, then?

VEIDT: Not at all. Some of my dearest friends are numbered amongst them. I wish them all nothing but luck in the years that lie ahead.

NOVA: In closing, you've often been referred to in the press as the world's smartest man. Is that true, and does it bother you?

VEIDT: No, that isn't true, but it's very flattering and I don't mind a bit. If somebody wants to call me the world's best-groomed man, then hey, that's okay too. (*Laughs*) No, no, I don't mind being the smartest man in the world. I just wish it wasn't this one. ◆

CHAPTER XII

5

A STRONGER LOVING WORLD

VEIDT. OF COURSE. WHO ELSE HAS THE INTELLIGENCE OR RESOURCES FOR TACHYON INTERFERENCE?

HMM. EIGHT GENERATORS THROUGHOUT ANTARCTICA, EIGHT IN ORBITING SATELLITES. IT DISPLAYS REMARKABLE FORESIGHT, DON'T YOU THINK?

UCCUK HUT

AFTER ALL, SINCE TACHYONS ONLY AFFECT ME, HE'S OBVIOUSLY ANTICIPATED MY POSSIBLE DISCOVERY OF HIS PLOT FOR SOME CONSIDERABLE TIME...

PLOT?

WAIT A MINUTE. I'VE BEEN HERE. THIS IS ANTARCTICA. THAT'S...

THAT'S ADRIAN'S FORTRESS.

A-ARE YOU SAYING SOMEONE PLANNED ...THAT ADRIAN PLANNED ALL THAT...THAT STUFF IN NEW YORK? THAT HE...THAT VEIDT...

YES. YES, HE KILLED BLAKE AND HALF NEW YORK.

EXCUSE ME, RORSCHACH. I'M INFORMING LAURIE NINETY SECONDS AGO.

RORSCHACH? JON, DON'T! DON'T START ALL YOUR CRAP NOW!

DID HE KILL THEM? DID VUH-VEIDT KILL ALL THOSE PUH-PEOPLE?

JON, ANSWER ME!

I-I'M SORRY. IT'S THESE TACHYONS. THEY'RE MUDDLING THINGS UP...

I'D BETTER FOLLOW HIM INSIDE.

NO! DON'T YOU DARE LEAVE ME OUT HERE!

JON, WAIT!

OH...

26

...DEAR.

11

13

16

I SAVED EARTH FROM *HELL.* NEXT, I'LL HELP HER TOWARDS *UTOPIA.* IT IS AS RAMESES SAID:

"CANAAN IS DEVASTATED, ASHKELON IS FALLEN, GEZER IS RUINED, YENOAM IS REDUCED TO NOTHING..."

"...ISRAEL IS DESOLATE AND HER SEED IS NO MORE, AND PALESTINE HAS BECOME A WIDOW FOR EGYPT..."

WAIT A MINUTE... "*NEXT*"? AFTER WHAT *YOU* DID? YOU CAN'T GET AWAY WITH *THAT...*

Panel 3:
"ALL THE COUNTRIES ARE *UNIFIED* AND *PACIFIED.*"

CAN'T GET AWAY WITH IT?

WILL YOU *EXPOSE* ME, UNDOING THE PEACE MILLIONS *DIED* FOR? *KILL* ME, RISKING SUBSEQUENT *INVESTIGATION*? MORALLY, YOU'RE IN *CHECKMATE,* LIKE BLAKE.

LET'S *COMPROMISE.*

WHAAT?

Panel 4:
LOGICALLY, I'M AFRAID HE'S *RIGHT.* EXPOSING THIS PLOT, WE DESTROY ANY CHANCE OF PEACE, DOOMING EARTH TO *WORSE* DESTRUCTION.

ON *MARS,* YOU DEMONSTRATED LIFE'S *VALUE.* IF WE WOULD PRESERVE LIFE *HERE,* WE MUST REMAIN *SILENT.*

Panel 5:
NEVER *TELL* ANYONE? W-WE REALLY HAVE TO *BUY* THIS?

JESUS, HE WAS *RIGHT.* ALL WE DID WAS *FAIL* TO STOP HIM SAVING EARTH.

JESUS.

HOW...HOW CAN *HUMANS* MAKE DECISIONS LIKE *THIS*? *WE'RE* DAMNED IF WE STAY *QUIET,* EARTH'S DAMNED IF WE *DON'T.* WE...

OKAY.

OKAY, COUNT ME IN. WE SAY NOTHING.

Panel 7:
JOKING, OF COURSE.

Panel 8:
RORSCHACH...?

RORSCHACH, *WAIT*! WHERE ARE YOU *GOING*? THIS IS TOO *BIG* TO BE *HARD-ASSED* ABOUT! WE HAVE TO COMPROMISE...

NO.

NOT EVEN IN THE FACE OF ARMA-GEDDON.

Panel 9:
NEVER COMPROMISE.

20

WHERE ARE YOU GOING?

BACK TO OWLSHIP. BACK TO AMERICA.

EVIL MUST BE PUNISHED.

PEOPLE MUST BE TOLD.

RORSCHACH...

YOU KNOW I CAN'T LET YOU DO THAT.

23

HUHHH.

OF COURSE. MUST PROTECT VEIDT'S NEW UTOPIA. ONE MORE BODY AMONGST FOUNDATIONS MAKES LITTLE DIFFERENCE.

WELL? WHAT ARE YOU WAITING FOR?

DO IT.

RORSCHACH....

DO IT!

HELLO, JON.

I WAS HOPING WE'D HAVE THE CHANCE TO TALK.

26

JON... I **KNOW** PEOPLE THINK ME CALLOUS, BUT I'VE MADE MYSELF **FEEL** EVERY **DEATH**. BY DAY I IMAGINE ENDLESS **FACES**. BY NIGHT...

WELL, I **DREAM**, ABOUT SWIMMING TOWARDS A HIDEOUS... NO. NEVER MIND. IT ISN'T **SIGNIFICANT**...

WHAT'S SIGNIFICANT IS THAT I **KNOW**. I **KNOW** I'VE STRUGGLED ACROSS THE BACKS OF MURDERED INNOCENTS TO SAVE HUMANITY... BUT **SOMEONE** HAD TO TAKE THE WEIGHT OF THAT AWFUL, NECESSARY CRIME.

I'D HOPED **YOU'D** UNDERSTAND, UNLIKE **RORSCHACH**...

YOU NEEDN'T CONSIDER RORSCHACH. I STRONGLY DOUBT HE'LL REACH CIVILIZATION.

...BUT YES, I UNDERSTAND, WITHOUT CONDONING OR CONDEMNING. HUMAN AFFAIRS CANNOT BE MY CONCERN. I'M **LEAVING** THIS GALAXY FOR ONE LESS **COMPLICATED**.

BUT YOU'D REGAINED INTEREST IN **HUMAN LIFE**...

YES, I HAVE. I THINK PERHAPS I'LL **CREATE** SOME.

GOODBYE, ADRIAN.

JON, WAIT, BEFORE YOU **LEAVE**...

I DID THE RIGHT THING, DIDN'T I? IT ALL WORKED OUT IN THE END.

"IN THE END"?

NOTHING ENDS, ADRIAN. NOTHING **EVER** ENDS.

JON? **WAIT!** WHAT DO YOU MEAN BY...

27

OOOHH, SO YOU FINALLY CAME **BACK**? WHAT, DID YOU GO TO **DIMENSION X** FOR 'EM? HM?

SEYMOUR, CHRIST, I DON'T KNOW ...

THREE MILLION NEW YORKERS DIED AND YOU WEREN'T ONE OF THEM.

31

It would be a
stronger world,
a stronger loving
world, to die in.

—John Cale

Quis custodiet ipsos custodes.

Who watches the watchmen?

—Juvenal, *Satires,* VI, 347
Quoted as the epigraph of the
Tower Commission Report, 1987

ALAN MOORE:

Starting where George Orwell left off, I began work on what eventually became WATCHMEN in 1984. I can't remember for certain, but I think it was probably some ludicrous notion that the book would be coming out the following year that led me to set the series in 1985. Anyway, it's now January 1988, and this current piece is the very last work that I expect to be doing upon WATCHMEN for the foreseeable future. We've written and drawn the comic. We've helped design the badges and approved the wristwatches. We've discussed the film and the role-playing games and given the nod to the T-shirts. We've done the British tour and the American press interviews. We've done the photo session where they asked us to pose as Adam West and Burt Ward, walking sideways up a wall on our Bat-rope. We've signed so many books that we're thinking of swapping names just to relieve the tedium, and every time we see that stupid, jaundiced, little smiling face with the red blood splash we get a crippling migraine. It's been four years since I started it, a year since I actually finished writing it, and only now am I starting to get any sort of perspective upon what it was we actually did.

It all began innocently enough, the initial impulse coagulating from a number of seemingly innocuous sources. Firstly, DC Comics were eager for me to write something else for them in addition to the monthly SWAMP THING. For my part, having taken SWAMP THING over from another writer "on the run" as it were, I've been forced to learn how to write full-length comic books at a breathless pace that leaves no time for proper planning or contemplation. Having formulated a few ideas about the possibilities of the American comic book during that heady, forty-issue rush, I was anxious to try them out in a new title that could be styled and designed from the ground upwards, and thus took up DC's offer with little prompting.

Next, there was a longstanding desire to work with Dave on something substantial. We've enjoyed our collaborations on the various "Future Shocks" that we turned out together for Britain's 2000 AD weekly, and had discussed the idea of approaching DC with a proposal for a series involving nostalgic favorites like the Martian Manhunter or the Challengers of the Unknown. While these proposals came to nothing in themselves, they did make our collaboration a logical move when we both found ourselves simultaneously looking for a new project to work on.

The final element was the plot and substance of the work itself, born from a lot of half-remembered preprofessional fantasies about how I'd write a comic book, given half a chance. In its simplest form, the notion was simply to take over a whole comic book continuity and all the characters in it, so that one writer could document the entire world without worrying about how his plans could be fitted in with the creators of the other titles his characters were currently appearing in. Regular comics, with their insistence upon rigid, cross-title continuity, present a lot of annoying limitations to the creator. The worst of these is that nothing can ever happen in any individual story that has any lasting effect on the world, since it is the same world inhabited by every other character in the company's line. Having a whole cast of characters in a self-contained world would solve these difficulties, and my original idea, for what it's worth, involved the characters of the MLJ-Archie Comic super-hero line, the Mighty Crusaders. This, restricted to idle fanboy musing as it was, has no special significance, save that it was fairly easy to make the conceptual leap to the characters of the defunct Charlton comics line once I heard that DC had acquired the rights to them.

On the following pages, you'll see extracts from the lengthy synopsis I wrote involving the Charlton characters...Captain Atom, The Blue Beetle and so on. One thing that becomes clear upon re-reading these early notes is that despite its eccentric flourishes of style and character, what we had here was a fairly straightforward super-hero story. Any super-heroes would have done.

This said, I'll admit to a certain disappointment when I learned that we couldn't use the Charlton characters after all. While it would be relatively easy to come up with original substitute characters, I felt that we'd be missing some of the poignance of the idea that went with having a long established continuity to lend nostalgic weight to the concept. It was only when I realized that if we were smart enough we could manufacture the appearance of a continuity stretching back years that the idea started to finally come together.

Bearing the above in mind and reading between the lines of the preliminary notes that follow, I think it's fairly easy to deduce our intentions as we sat down to craft WATCHMEN issue one: we wanted to do a novel and unusual super-hero comic that allowed us the opportunity to try out a few new storytelling ideas along the way. What we ended up with was substantially more than that.

Somewhere along the way, in between the material we were working with and the new narrative techniques we were attempting, something began to happen that we hadn't really anticipated. The more we looked at the story, the more depth became apparent. The greater our understanding of the subliminal background details that we were using became, the more those details became integrated with the storyline, acting as a sort of meta-continuity that eventually equaled the plot in its importance to the finished work. As we fleshed out the characters from the loose talk and wild ideas contained in the following outline, we found ourselves led into progressively deeper waters: it wasn't enough to describe the particular circumstances in the life of a Rorschach or a Dr. Manhattan without considering their politics, their sexuality, their philosophy and all of the factors in their world that had shaped those things. Thus, from a relatively conventional nuclear-powered super-hero we found ourselves wandering into some post-Einsteinian quantum ruminations about time. The same thing applied to the disturbing moral territory we came to from the starting point of a standard masked urban vigilante. We couldn't discuss these characters without discussing the world that had shaped them, and we couldn't discuss that world without in some way referring to our own, if only obliquely. In this way, what started life as merely a more cynical and baroque take upon the Justice League of America and their ilk suddenly found itself standing in the public marketplace of conventional mainstream fiction, dressed only in a cloak and a pair of brightly-colored tights. Thematically, we began to realize that we were playing in a new neighborhood, just as in terms of storytelling we began to understand that we were playing a relatively new game.

This was both exhilarating and slightly alarming. On the one hand, there was the excitement of seeing something like the Dr. Manhattan episode or Chapter Five's "Fearful Symmetry" actually work. There was the weird delight of stumbling across some previously unheard quotation or fragment of obscure information that would fit with supernatural precision into what we were attempting to construct. On the other hand, there was the mounting suspicion (at least on my part) that we might have bitten off more than we could chew, that we might not be able to resolve all these momentous strands of narrative and meaning that seemed to be springing up wherever we looked, that we might be left at the end of the day with a big, messy, steaming bowl of semiotic spaghetti.

The subtle creative stresses and pressures involved in this sort of project are such that you're not really aware of them at the time in more than the vaguest sense. It's only now, twelve months after triumphantly typing "The End" in big, underlined capitals beneath panel seven on page twenty-eight of my script for issue twelve that I realize how dazed a state I'd spent that year in, as if I'd been slam dancing with a bunch of rhinos and the concussion was only just starting to clear up.

On the whole, I think we pulled it off. Even if I'm wrong and it was all just spaghetti after all, I'm still very satisfied with WATCHMEN on a personal level. It's taught me things about storytelling that have opened up a whole new range of possibilities for the future, now that I've had time and hindsight with which to assimilate what we did. It made me think about issues in the real world which I might otherwise have avoided considering quite so intensely. Finally, and not without some irony, it has satisfied my appetite for super-heroes. Like the bottle of perfume in the story, my nostalgia for the genre cracked and shattered somewhere along the way and all the sweet old musk inside just leaked out and evaporated. For better or worse, the ordinary nontelepathic, unmutated and slightless humanoids hanging out on their anonymous street corner of WATCHMEN have come to seem more precious and interesting than the movers of rivers and shakers of planets. I wish the super-hero well in whatever capable hands guide his flight in future, but for my part I'm eager to get back to earth.

And that's it. Four years and nearly four hundred pages later, it's finally over. On the following pages you see the first clumsy and faltering steps along the track, and although they bear little resemblance to the steroid brute that eventually broke the ribbon on the finish line, I hope that they'll add to your enjoyment of the race.

Human or otherwise.

Alan Moore
Northampton
January 1988

<u>WORLD</u>

GEODESIC DOMES
REAR ENGINED ELECTRIC CARS (LIGHTWEIGHT POLYACETYLENE BATTERIES
                                REQUIRING RARE LITHIUM FOR MANUFACTURE)
DOUBLE BREASTED SUITS
UNUSUAL FAST FOODS
UNUSUAL FADS, ADDICTIONS
NO DISEASE
(NO POVERTY)
WIDESPREAD FEELINGS OF INADEQUACY, LACK OF MOTIVATION
PIRATE, MEDIAEVAL, WESTERN RATHER THAN S.F. MOVIES ETC?
LESS SEXUAL RESTRAINT
AIRSHIPS
SUBMARINE FREIGHTERS
EARTH ORBIT = ANTARCTICA
ANTARCTICA = RICH KIDS HOLIDAY PLAYGROUND (MAYBE O2'S HQ HERE)
WEATHER CONTROL

ALAN —
THOUGHT YOU MIGHT
LIKE THIS. THIS IS
THE FIRST VISUAL I'D
FEEL LIKE SHOWING
ANYONE ELSE!

(opposite page)
Early visuals of
Dr. Manhattan,
the N.Y.P.D. and
the Comedian.
Handwritten notes
are Gibbons' thoughts
upon reading
Moore's outline.

(left) First group shot.

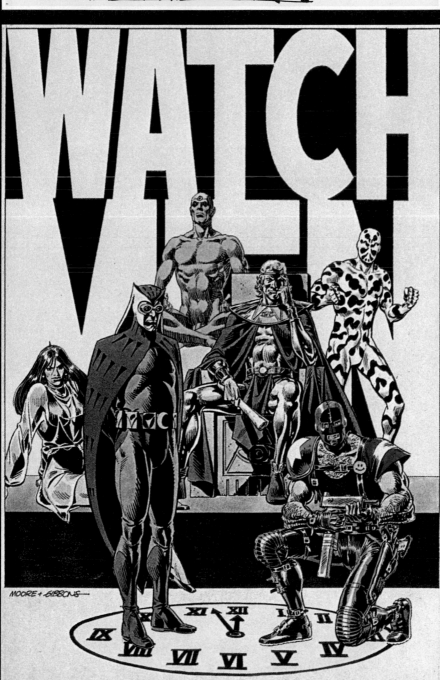

Finished visual,
colored as a guide
for John Higgins.

JON AT 16

= HYDROGEN

CAPTAIN ATOM (DOC MANHATTAN)

BOWIE
ELRIC
ALIENATED, ISOLATED
MYSTICAL HERMIT
PERMANENT 25 GOING ON 44

SEES WORLD AS
SUB-ATOMIC SYSTEM

THUNDERBOLT (OZYMANDIAS)

10 x HUMAN INTELLIGENCE
YOUNG 37 WILL LIVE TO 150
REDFORD, KENNEDY
POPULAR CELEBRITY
RICH
PERFECT
LONER
'PRESCIENT' THRU INTELLIGENCE

SEES WORLD AS
ORGANISM WITH HIM
AT CENTRE

DOCTOR
MANHATTAN!

NITE OWL

BLUE BEETLE (NITE OWL)

ORDINARY, FALLIBLE, HUMAN
HEROIC, THO NOT NATURALLY COURAGEOUS
SCIENTIST
DEEP THINKING, CONCERNED, DOUBTING
'VETERAN' HERO, MALADJUSTED
SUBSTITUTE FOR ORIGINAL
   NEWMAN, FURILLO

DOESN'T KNOW
HOW HE SEES
   WORLD

COMEDIAN

1940   1966   1971   1985
AGE 16 AGE 42 AGE 47 AGE 61

PEACEMAKER (THE COMEDIAN)

DIRTY FIGHTER, RETIRED
ATHLETIC, ANIMAL
(DIRTY HARRY?)(MEETS NICK FURY?)
(MEETS HANNIBAL OF 'A-TEAM'?)
'SERIOUS PEOPLE'
WORKMANLIKE

HAS NO TIME
OR INTEREST FOR
'SEEING' WORLD

(left) Color guide sketches of the Minutemen.

(above) Finished group shot of the Minutemen from DC WHO'S WHO #4

(above) Final group shot, from signature plate for French limited edition portfolio.

(below) T-shirt design adapted from DC WHO'S WHO #5.

(top rows) Roughs and finished promotional artwork.

(bottom row) Sketches of first cover and unused covers for later issues, predating second script.

(above, left) Cover for Mayfair Games role-playing module.

(above, right) Page for British convention booklet.

Cover for French reprint album. Color by Higgins.

DAVE GIBBONS:

The hour is late; all deeds are done, all plans revealed and, since the writer's gone home early, it falls to me to make the final entry in this crank file. But rest easy, no last-minute revelations lurk here, threatening to upset what has gone before, only a few closing credits and a fond farewell before I clock off myself.

The preceding pages have given you a glimpse of what Alan and I put down on paper during the planning of WATCHMEN, but what they cannot capture, of course, are the hours of thought and conversation that went into the thing nor the sheer pleasure we derived from the collaboration. Even though the pressure became quite intense towards the end, at no time was there ever anything else I would rather have been doing and I'm pleased to record that, though we are both possessed of considerable egos, a cross word never passed between us in all the time it took. Lest I become maudlin, let me just leave you with an image of us as some sort of bizarre tennis doubles team, each sensing when to step in and when to stand back, mutually determined to knock that ball back and, above all, not to let our partner down.

In sporting mood, this would seem an appropriate point at which to mention the other members of the team, as it were, without whose enthusiasm and commitment the ball still could easily have been fumbled.

Foremost, of course, is John Higgins, whose coloring never failed to amaze and delight us. Usually the first person to read each issue, his comments were eagerly awaited and the insight and understanding he brought to his work made his contribution an enrichment not to be underestimated. His Tuesday night visits with colored photostats for my "approval" were also a great excuse to open a couple of beers and shoot the breeze. Thanks, John.

Richard Bruning, at DC Comics, gave valuable support and advice. Through his expertise, our rough designs were translated into the polished graphics which graced the project and, together with Julia Sabbagh, he concocted sympathetic layouts around the copy and illustrations we provided for the various text features. Our special thanks to them and to everyone else at DC whose diligence enhanced the final product.

Thanks also to Bob Chapman of Graphitti Designs (whose calls from California must already have paid for an entire satellite) for his efforts to ensure that this edition came as close to being a "dream book" as humanly possible.

And, of course, our thanks to you, dear reader, for the enthusiasm and commitment you have shown by reading this far. We know it hasn't been easy, but we hope it's been worthwhile. As a dedicated WATCHMEN reader myself (though for the first couple of readings of each issue suffering the unique disadvantage of having no pictures to help me) I've always found Alan's writing challenging and inspirational, and never more so than in his script for the "Dr. Manhattan on Mars" issue, where the good Doctor addresses what I feel is the central question posed by the series: "Who makes the world?"

Well, I'm no metaphysician but, if pushed for an answer, I'd say that it's Planning, People, and just Plain Luck that are responsible, though not necessarily in that order. In our story, as Dr. Manhattan ponders the riddle, he conjures up a convoluted structure of his own, by way of metaphor; similarly, as I attempt to place the last delicate spire on the complex microcosm that we have created, it is only the factor of "luck" that yet remains to be considered. And luck we most certainly have had, nearly all of the good variety, though to catalog here all the chance, coincidence and serendipity that has accompanied the genesis of Watchmen would probably fill another 48-page appendix and the hands of our blood-drenched clock are already edging perilously close to their final deadline.

Suffice it to say that, proud though we are of this work of fiction, we humbly acknowledge that the truth is infinitely more wonderful; depressing though it is to consider that Richard Nixon's signature is on the moon, the fact that there really is a smiley face on the planet Mars is strangely heartening.

Keep smiling.

Dave Gibbons
St. Albans
January 1988   *From the introduction to the Graphitti Designs edition*